QUILT
New Zealand

ACKNOWLEDGMENTS

My heartfelt thanks to the sponsors of this, the first national juried quiltmaking competition:

Enzed Sewing Ltd, Velcro (NZ) Ltd, Spring Industries Inc., Molnlycke Sewing Threads, English Sewing (NZ) Ltd, Verlag Aenne Burda, Scovill (NZ) Ltd, General Plastics (NZ) Ltd, Swaffield Print Ltd, General Products, Pako Handwerken BV, Ellis Fibre Processing Ltd, Kiyohara Taiwan Ltd, Ackroyd and Adams. Without their generous sponsorship this competition would not have been.

To Peter and Rinny Gordon of Enzed Sewing Ltd for their unfailing faith in New Zealand quiltmakers, for their vision in conceiving the competition, and their friendship and belief in me.

To my husband John, and son Matthew, who have been somewhat neglected and have learnt to live with chaos.

To fellow judges Sharyn Squier Craig and Ren Olykan for their perception and impartiality.

To my faithful staff at Patches of Ponsonby, who have allowed me the time to devote to this project.

To Trina Yeatts, my patient typist.

To Maggie and Barbara, for their friendship and encouragement.

To the quiltmakers of New Zealand, whose talents and abilities continue to stimulate and fascinate me. Without this marvellous band of creative people this book would not have been.

FRONT COVER: 'Putanga O Te Ra' by Gwen Wanigasekera
BACK COVER: Detail of 'Migration' by Barbara Bilyard

PUBLISHED by New House Publishers Ltd
P.O.Box 33–376, Takapuna, Auckland 9, New Zealand.

ISBN 1 86946 012 X

First published 1991

© 1991. Enzed Sewing Ltd

Printed in Hong Kong
Design by Suellen Allen

QUILT
New Zealand

TEXT: D I A N E   D O L A N   PHOTOGRAPHY: J O H N   D O L A N

in association with
ENZED SEWING LIMITED

NEW HOUSE PUBLISHERS

FOREWORD

Quiltmaking in New Zealand has a relatively short history. Although New Zealand women are renowned for their home dressmaking skills, it has only been in the past decade that they have turned their talents to the fine art of patchwork and quilting. The reasons for our lack of quilting history may be various. For many years, our fashion industry lagged behind that of our overseas counterparts; import tariffs, expensive raw materials, transportation and local labour costs resulted in the high prices of the indigenous garment industry, and women tended to be more traditionally motivated as devoted homemakers. The past fifteen years have seen remarkable changes. The workforce now has a much higher percentage of women employees, removal of tariffs has resulted in an influx of relatively cheap fashion garments and labour-saving devices, leisure time is now regarded more highly, and time-out for mothers, wives and working women is common practice. The necessity to sew for oneself and one's family is of lesser importance. Our creative sewing skills have needed another outlet. The upsurge of quiltmaking in the United States and Canada has been reflected in New Zealand, but rather than an upsurge it has been an awakening.

New Zealand women seem to share a passion for fabric, for its colour, its texture, its tactile nature and its ability to be manipulated. Quiltmaking has been a natural source and progression for the sewing skills so many of us acquired as children. The very nature of quiltmakers has made the transition from more traditional home sewing to that of a creative and decorative art form, one of pleasure and satisfaction. The willingness to share ideas and skills appears to be unique to this art and creates a warmth and friendship highly regarded amongst quiltmakers.

Our isolation as a nation is reflected in our quiltmaking, both locally and nationally. Nationally we display a diverse range of styles, colours and innovation. The bright, clean colours of our country are frequently abundant in the quilts we exhibit. The willingness of our quiltmakers to experiment in technique and design has resulted in the rapid development of a body of artists of world class. On a more local level, quilts from the densely populated northern regions of New Zealand have a high technical quality and traditional elements indicative of the availability and diversity of tutors. The isolation and grandeur of our more southern locations is reflected in the willingness of those quiltmakers to experiment with colour and design and in the production of highly innovative individual works.

New Zealand quiltmaking has, more recently, begun to move away from the traditional utility bed quilt projects towards highly decorative and creative wall hangings. Fabric, by its very nature, drapes with a sensuous softness, allows for movement, is forgiving in its management and workability and has a texture and flexibility difficult to emulate in other mediums.

Keen to recognise the talents of our quiltmakers were Peter and Rinny Gordon of Enzed Sewing Limited, the major suppliers of haberdashery to the New Zealand home sewing market. As early as 1972, Enzed Sewing imported quiltmaking supplies to tempt our creative population. Unfortunately, this innovative company was well ahead of the times and these products were soon regarded as "dead stock". Undeterred, Peter and Rinny Gordon shared a continuing fascination with quiltmaking. In 1986, acknowledging the value of quilts as an art form, they commissioned Libby Shallard and Judy Hewin to produce a wall hanging as the major feature for the board room of their new company headquarters. In 1987 the Gordons attended the opening of a private quilt exhibition in a small South Auckland community. The enthusiasm and support of the large contingent of locals present surprised and captivated the couple. At that time, the retail trade was experiencing a downturn and the industry was depressed. The Gordons wanted to stimulate a positive response from their customers and to lift morale in the trade. Bouncing ideas off each other and a retailing customer, Dianne Duff, a nationwide quiltmaking contest was conceived. Rinny enthusiastically followed up the idea and contacted Barbara Bilyard, the then president of the Auckland Patchworkers and Quilters Guild. The idea of a juried show was mooted, prize monies discussed, and with the interest and/or cajoling of suppliers to Enzed Sewing Limited, the richest purse to be offered in New

Zealand arts and crafts was decided. The Enzed Sewing 1990 Nationwide Quiltmaking Competition was born.

New Zealand quiltmakers embraced the competition with a willingness and enthusiasm which delighted the Gordons. Regional exhibitions were held in fourteen centres throughout New Zealand. From these, seventy one quilts were selected for final judging and exhibition at the Aotea Centre in Auckland. Quilts were entered in four categories: Traditional Bed Quilts, Traditional Wall Quilts, Contemporary Bed Quilts, Contemporary Wall Quilts. Regional judges Ren Olykan and Diane Dolan were surprised by the strong interest in the Contemporary Wall Quilt section which accounted for more than half the quilts viewed throughout New Zealand and in the finals exhibition. Tutor and quilt judge Sharon Squier Craig from San Diego, U.S.A., the Chief Adjudicator for the competition, stated 'I am very impressed with the finalist quilts. The workmanship and the technical skills of many have absolutely astounded me. They are every bit as good in terms of workmanship and quality as anything I have seen in the States.'

The following pages are devoted to the talented body of New Zealand quiltmakers who were successful in reaching the finals of this most prestigious competition. Their quilts display an artistry and skill never before seen, on this scale, within New Zealand. From the creative magnificence of our top contemporary quilt artists to the traditional methods employed by the strong band of hobbyist quiltmakers, I am sure readers will be well-satisfied when dipping into this collection.

DIANE DOLAN
JULY 1990

CONTENTS

The reproduction of quilts in this book is not indicative of scale relative to one another. Please refer to actual measurements indicated below each quilt.

TRADITIONAL
BED QUILTS

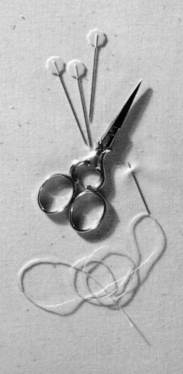

As a child, Hazel Collinson received parcels of fabric from her mother as Christmas presents. 'She influenced me. I have always worked with fabric. I worked in the clothing industry for 22 years. Now I teach the unemployed to sew for both pleasure and commercial purposes.' Fifteen years ago Hazel taught her daughter how to English piece. 'My mother had made "blanket" quilts from old clothing, not like we know quilts now. They were heavy and dull, a necessity, and batted with a woollen blanket. Although I dabbled in a minor way, I thought quiltmaking was an unimportant thing.' That was before Hazel attended a Rose City Quilters' 'Tote and Gloat' and was overcome by the beauty of quilts. The year was 1985 and she was prompted to join a local evening class in beginners patchwork and quilting. Her tutor, Pene Williamson, suggested to Hazel that the art was just her thing, 'and it was. I have been quiltmaking ever since. I really like the people involved, I have made lovely friends. I enjoy attending symposiums and workshops. The things I make do not go out of fashion, they are permanent.' Hazel chose to use a half-made block from a workshop she had attended to make this quilt. Initially she planned to make a single bed quilt but felt the block size was too large. 'I made five blocks then realised that I needed four half blocks for the sides and four more for the corners. It took me a month to piece the top. I chose Flying Geese to border the quilt. I like the sharpness of the design – I could sew these until 1.30 am and wonder where the time had gone. Quilting took care of itself, although I took some time to decide on the Clamshell design. It had to be something that related to the sea. My quilt reflects boat lights on dark waters with birds following for scraps of food.'

TIMELESS NIGHTS

Hazel Collinson
Paraparaumu Beach

WINNER

TRADITIONAL
BED QUILT

260cm by 234cm

Cotton fabrics, low loft polyester batting, machine-pieced, hand-appliqued centres, hand-quilted.

Anne Crampton
Nelson

203cm by 177cm

Cotton fabrics, furnishing fabrics,
wool batting, hand-appliqued,
machine-pieced, hand-quilted.

Anne Crampton wished to make a memorable quilt to celebrate the marriage of her son and daughter-in-law. The lucky couple chose to have Anne make an applique quilt and the design 'Techny Chimes' was selected from a 1985 *Quilters Newsletter Magazine*. The quilt was to fit a waterbed, which meant Anne spent some time modifying the pattern. Once the central applique pattern was completed, Anne added the Flying Geese borders and the rest just happened – it had to fit the size of the bed. Anne also appliqued, pieced and quilted four matching pillowslips. The inspiration for the colour scheme was from the furnishing fabric used in the quilt. Anne feels 'the applique pattern used echoes the soft flowing lines of this fabric'. Not everything went as planned – 'The Flying Geese section of the quilt was started at a quilting weekend held at Lake Rotoiti, Nelson. I thought I would complete it in a morning, but found that using a furnishing fabric with a craft cotton made the going difficult. I finished one side and gave up. I made a teddy bear instead.' Seven years ago, Anne attended a beginners course in patchwork and quilting, run by Anne Patrick. 'I was hooked immediately. Anne has been a real inspiration to me.' Initially, Anne Crampton made a few traditional quilts but has moved on to wall hangings, something she enjoys more. Anne is an addicted fabric collector, her first love being upholstery and furnishing fabrics. Her husband says, 'She stays up and works half the night to meet deadlines.'

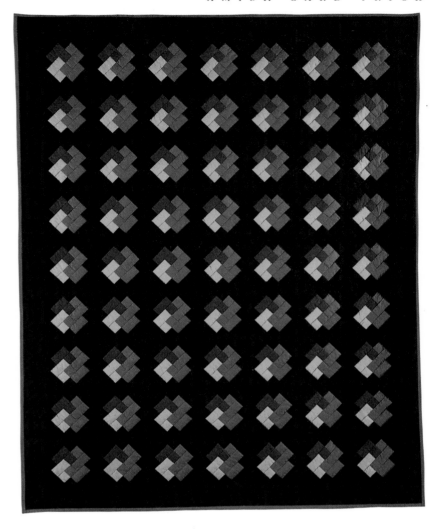

Valerie Devlin has been quiltmaking for more than twenty years, initially inspired to begin the art after viewing quilts made by residents of a girls' home. Although self-taught, she decided to attend a local beginners patchwork and quilting class in 1983. 'I would look at pictures and become inspired. I didn't read the instructions and it wasn't until I attended this class that I realised quilting stitches should be small.' In 1985 Valerie decided to give up quiltmaking. 'I started again two years ago. I now do much finer work. In particular I make more effort with quilting. I also enjoy my results more now.' Valerie purchased the fabrics for her Card Trick quilt on 1 February, which meant she had only four weeks in which to complete the project. 'I finished the quilt at 3 pm on the deadline day. It required long hours of hard work to complete it.' Valerie combined her love of Amish colours and the desire to make a Card Trick quilt for this project. Piecing was completed by a quick strip method. Quilting late into the night on a black background resulted in Valerie visiting an optician and purchasing her first pair of glasses. She says of her quilt, 'Although Card Trick is an old pattern it was not traditionally used by the Amish. I made this quilt for a teenage boy and I chose my colours to give it a modern feel.' She continues to make quilts 'because I love colour, design and art. Fabric is what I love to work with. Although I have worked on original pictorial banners, traditional is the area in which I prefer to work.'

AMISH CARD TRICK

Valerie Devlin
Palmerston North

176cm by 140cm

Cotton fabrics, wool batting,
machine-pieced, hand-quilted.

SCRAP TUMBLERS

Dorothy Doherty
Mangateretere

278cm by 190cm

Cotton fabrics, polyester batting,
hand-pieced, hand-quilted.

Four years ago, Dorothy Doherty attended a course in beginners patchwork and quilting. 'I knew I would get hooked so I waited until I had time to devote to quilting.' Since those first lessons Dorothy has worked, for the most part, on her own. She decided to make a scrap quilt. 'I have always wanted to make a scrap one patch quilt. To me scrap quilts are what patchwork is all about. The Tumblers design appealed to me – I like the shape. Planning was fairly haphazard. I looked for a patch that blended with those around it. I wanted to achieve a subtle progression from light to dark. With quilting I did not wish to do the usual thing. I tried various ideas but eventually decided to follow the natural diagonals of the Tumblers design.' Dorothy was able to supplement her scrap collection with travellers' samples from the fifties and sixties, which belonged to a friend. Living with two artistic people, Dorothy is delighted with the satisfaction and pleasure she gets from quiltmaking. 'Colour and art have always interested me. Now I can do something that gives me creative satisfaction.' Dorothy has always worked within traditional bounds but hopes 'to try something small, to break away', in the near future.

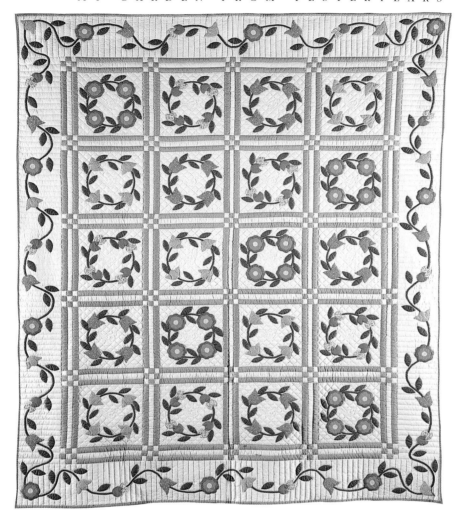

Gloria Green began quiltmaking five years ago after an ongoing period of ill health. While working towards a full recovery, she felt 'there was something I wanted and needed to do. I saw a photograph of a quilt and collected all the library books I could find on the subject. These I read for about three months and then embarked on my first quilt. I made a few quilts but felt I was not growing, I couldn't learn enough from books. I attended an applique course which really inspired me and helped my progress.' A 1984 *Country Quilts* magazine provided Gloria with the impetus to make 'My Garden from Yesteryears'. Featured in the magazine was a quilt completed from a series of old applique blocks a woman had purchased at a garage sale. Gloria says, 'I was intrigued by the article, and by the fact that the blocks were made by an unknown quiltmaker. While making this quilt, I thought about what the quiltmaker had envisioned. I would like to think that my finished quilt is similar to what she had in mind.' Gloria, a qualified machinist, worked on this project for a period of three and a half years. She was happy to have a project she could carry with her or one she could work on in front of the fire on cold winter evenings. During this period she completed at least another ten quilts. The Quiltmaking Competition encouraged her to complete this one. Gloria is currently experimenting with colour and design, an area into which she has only begun to delve. She also plans to continue making traditional quilts, and further explore the Amish colour palette, a special love of hers. 'I am particularly influenced by the Papatoetoe Group I attend and by my husband, who is my strongest and most constructive critic. I have to keep quiltmaking. I need to justify all the fabric and the books I have. Also, I want to leave quilts to my children and my grandchildren.'

MY GARDEN FROM YESTERYEARS

Gloria Green
Auckland

215cm by 180cm

Cotton fabrics, lofted polyester batting, hand-appliqued, machine-pieced, hand-quilted.

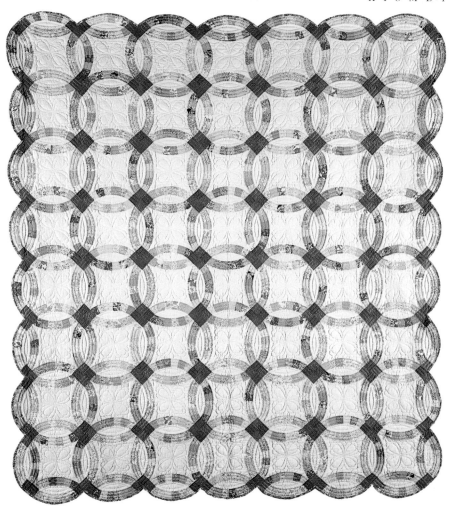

'My family were delighted when I finished quilting this quilt. The quilting frame was removed from the dining room and we could eat at the table again,' said Helen. 'I chose to make a traditional Double Wedding Ring quilt as I am amazed at the possibilities for this beautiful design. The effect I desired was a soft-coloured quilt with interlocking rings. This is only one of many Double Wedding Ring quilts I wish to make.' Helen, an inveterate fabric collector, loves 'scrappy'-looking quilts and will happily use large numbers from her collection to get the desired effect. 'I used more than 50 print fabrics to make the rings. My background fabric, a very pale icy green, ran out. I was short by only six centres. I was unable to purchase more and in the end used a hand-dyed fabric a friend gave me. It is not quite the same'. Helen worked on the quilt for about six months with only a couple of small projects in progress at the same time. She first learnt patchwork and quilting whilst living in Canada. Initially self-taught, she attended lessons on her return to New Zealand, 'to make sure I was doing it the right way. I learnt not to hand-quilt 6 oz batting.' Helen taught beginners patchwork for several years before starting work in a patchwork shop two and a half years ago. 'The shop environment has broadened my horizons and made me much more aware of print fabrics and of colours. I am constantly inspired by those around me.'

KISMET

Helen Harford
Whangaparaoa

250cm by 222cm

Machine-pieced, hand-quilted,
cotton fabrics, wool batting.

SUCH FUN

Marie Johnson
Napier

270cm by 225cm

Cotton fabrics, furnishing fabrics,
wool batting, hand-pieced,
hand-quilted.

The urgent need to replace her existing quilt which was rapidly reaching the end of its life was all the encouragement Marie Johnson needed to begin this quilt. 'A scrap quilt provided an excellent reason to use up some of my mounting stocks of fabric and, of course, a great excuse to purchase yet more.' A photograph in *Quilting Today* was Marie's source of inspiration. She so enjoyed combining all the colours and fabrics that she overshot the number of twelve inch blocks she required, by eight. These are currently being made into cushions to match the quilt. Marie completely hand-made her quilt and quilting was completed on a hoop. She says, 'I am grateful for an Olfa Cutter and Board, a Bias Square and a Yours Truly Template – these all made for speed and accuracy.' This is the largest quilt Marie has tackled. She doubts that she would make another quilt of this size. 'To me, my quilt represents a most enjoyable nine months, the fun of receiving fabrics from friends to include in the blocks, and the challenge of quilting such a large area.' Marie commenced patchwork and quilting classes when she retired at the age of 60. Eight years later, she still attends weekly classes with the same tutor, something she thoroughly enjoys.

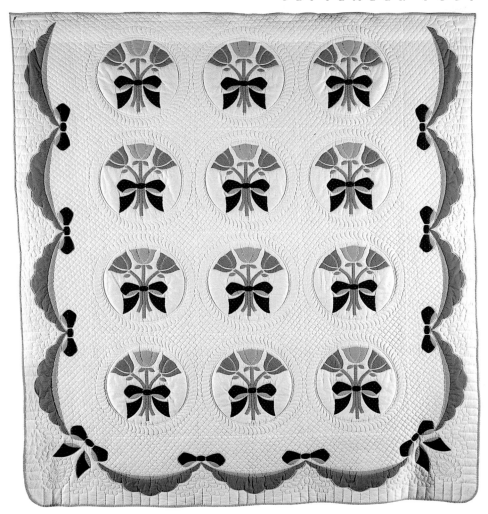

'September Posy' is the first applique quilt Margery McCarthy has made. She says, 'I made my quilt to express my joy of spring and as a tribute to my mother, grandmother and great-grandmother who taught, encouraged and inspired me to use my hands.' A tulip stencil design caught Margery's imagination, and with some modification became the basis of her applique block. The addition of the bow finalised the design-image she desired. Applique was completed by the freezer paper method. Colours came from a piece of bone china that Margery particularly admires. While working on the applique blocks, she constantly thought about the shape of the finished pieces. 'I wanted another shape and thought constantly about an oval. I decided on a feather quilting design and my square became a circle.' Margery was most grateful for the assistance of her husband while she was rushing towards her deadline. He became a 'working mother'. 'He cooked the dinner and was happy to help. When I became frustrated and said I wasn't going to complete the quilt he would say, "You mean I did all the cooking for nothing?" On I would quilt! Some days I quilted for fourteen hours, but usually they were twelve-hour days for the last month. My fingers blistered inside my thimbles. It became quite a desperate effort to complete the quilt.' Quiltmaking gives Margery an enormous amount of pleasure. 'I love colour. In the past I bought odd balls of brightly coloured wool and wondered what to do with them. When I discovered quiltmaking, it began to make sense.'

SEPTEMBER POSY

Margery McCarthy
Paraparaumu Beach

220cm by 198cm

Cotton fabrics, lofted polyester batting, hand-appliqued, hand-quilted.

17

SARONGS II

Juliet Taylor
Auckland

MERIT AWARD

250cm by 230cm

Machine-pieced, hand-quilted,
100% cotton sarong and
batik fabrics, wool batting.

An addicted fabric collector, Juliet fell in love with, and began purchasing sarong and batik fabrics while living in Malaysia in 1974. The desire to make a quilt from these fabrics began to dominate her thoughts during 1988 when friends who travelled to the East returned with yet more sarongs. Juliet says, 'I have always loved sarongs and batiks as compositions. The richness of the fabrics are what I wanted to show so I chose a simple repeating block which I bordered with black, a colour which almost always appears in these fabrics. Because sarong and batik prints are large, the pieces needed to be large. The Clamshell pattern was ideal for this especially as it is frequently seen in the East in decorative arts.' Initially it was the intention of the artist to use only 'hot' colours, thus continuing the theme of the East but, says Juliet, 'I got bored as usual so I threw in some cooler ones.' This is the second in a series of Sarong quilts made by Juliet – the first was exhibited at the American Quilters Society Annual Show (1990) at Paducah, Kentucky. She continued the theme as she felt she was on the right track, but her first attempt lacked sophistication. Also, as with dedicated 'fabricaholics', Juliet estimates she had only used 10 percent of the fabrics she had collected.

TRADITIONAL
WALL QUILTS

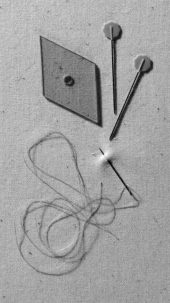

A quiltmaker for the past seven years, Jenny Barker hopes she lives long enough to complete all the quilts she wishes to make. She has a particular interest in applique, traditional piecing and design. Making 'Christmas Heirloom' is something Jenny has always wanted to do. She saw the setting of a completely different quilt and knew instantly that that was how she wanted to construct her quilt. 'I wanted every aspect of Christmas in the quilt. The centre of my Christmas is the nativity, therefore I made it the centre of my project. I see Christmas in three areas – religious, with the nativity, angel and candle blocks; giving, with Santa, toys and parcels; and family, with the fireplace and the tree.' Jenny had no desire to use what is usually thought of as traditional Christmas colours but wanted the quilt to look olde worlde. 'I chose no brights. I used a lot of dull pinks, reds and greens in the quilt. The green and brown checked fabric offered me a real challenge.' Some of the blocks were inspired by pictures in magazines but most were designed by Jenny or her friends. Love of tradition encouraged the use of particular patchwork techniques to give detail. The Christmas stocking is strip-pieced and the angel has seminole around her skirt. Embroidery was used to embellish and enhance the blocks. Jenny says, 'I look forward to sharing my quilt with family and friends at Christmas time, and I particularly look forward to the day when I can tell my grandchildren about it and about Christmas.' When asked why she quilts, Jenny's daughter Jackie commented, 'Mum is very in tune with her environment and inspired by it and by nature, but basically her obsession with quiltmaking drives her.'

CHRISTMAS HEIRLOOM

Jenny Barker
Orewa

167cm square

Cotton fabrics, wool batting, hand-appliqued, machine-pieced, hand-quilted, hand-embroidered.

Pam Carter
Auckland

157cm by 198cm

Cotton fabrics, wool batting,
machine-pieced, hand-quilted.

Pam Carter had dabbled in many crafts before discovering quilting. 'I just knew it was right. I have always sewn. I enjoy fabrics and colour, and find that quiltmaking allows me to follow these pleasures.' Pam began by learning from books and still uses the velveteen corduroy cushions she attempted first. Night classes at the local high school provided Pam with the stimulus 'to get going and finish something'. 'I did not achieve a great deal at that time but I was happy just to be there, to be part of the energy of people creating.' She feels that the real impetus to her developing as a quiltmaker was provided by a dream. 'I dreamt about a butterfly that was a woman and I got out of bed especially to draw it. I made this into a wallhanging, using the stained-glass technique. I entered it into a local show which Malcolm Harrison critiqued. I was delighted that he had written two pages about my piece. He made me start believing in myself – it was a great boost to my confidence.' Initially Pam worked only in solid colours, preferring bold brights. Although she now often uses prints, she feels that solids will always be her first love. In 'Twisted Yellow Path', Pam used the traditional Round the Twist pattern, choosing to construct it by Trudie Hughes' template free method. She made several copies of the graphed quilt and played with colour before making her final fabric selection. She says, 'This quilt had been in my head for eighteen months or so. I wanted to make a bold statement and chose to use bright solids. This is unusual in that this traditional pattern is normally worked in two colours only.'

'The bias binding used in Celtic work must have no beginning or ending. Where the binding crosses each other it must go in a sequence of under one and over the next. This, to me, represents the never-ending family lifeline. I am of Celtic heritage – thus it is an appropriate wallhanging to make.' Instructions in a magazine for a cathedral window pin-cushion is what hooked Vonda Clarke into the world of quiltmaking, in 1983. The following year Vonda attended a beginners course, hand-making her first bed quilt. She says, 'I have never done a lot of traditional work. Although I enjoy learning traditional techniques, I am more interested in making contemporary quilts, especially wallhangings. I love to sew and love fabric. Combining both in a creative way gives me a lot of pleasure. My mother taught me to sew, I taught my mother to do patchwork.'

CELTIC APPLIQUE

Vonda Clarke
Hamilton

70cm square

Cotton fabrics, needled polyester batting, hand-appliqued, hand-quilted.

Robyn Croft
Auckland

67cm by 57cm

Hand-appliqued, hand-quilted,
cotton fabrics, wool batting.

'I just made this quilt because I wanted to. I enjoy working with the heart-shape and it appears often, in different ways, in my work. I just love hearts.' Heavily influenced by Roberta Horton, who she regards as a most professional quiltmaker and teacher, Robyn is presently working on Afro-style quilts and especially enjoys working with bright colours. Robyn stated, 'I never do nothing – there is always something on the go.' She has made about 40 quilts and has as many in her head or under the bed, unquilted. Although Robyn prefers to view contemporary quilts, she tends to work in the more traditional vein. As the owner of a patchwork shop in the early days of quilting in New Zealand, Robyn taught beginners patchwork for three and a half years. She feels she stood still in this period as she did not have time to make exciting quilts. She now enjoys quiltmaking much more. 'I feel you don't grow in your artistry overnight. It is a gradual process and it happens by exposure to the teaching of other artists and your environment.'

'There is nothing complicated or complex about my work, there is no reason for doing it other than pure pleasure. If I still like the quilt after the piecing stage, it gets quilted. This one passed the test.' Both quilts were inspired by glimpses of antique quilts in American decorating magazines. Robyn says, 'These two quilts are not truly representative of the work I currently do.'

LOVE YOUR MAMMY

Robyn Croft
Auckland

132cm by 104cm

Machine-pieced, hand-quilted, cotton fabrics with the odd exception, double layer 80/20 cotton batting.

Heather Harding
Wellington

70cm square

Machine-pieced, hand-quilted,
cotton fabrics, lofted polyester
batting.

Five years ago, while driving home from a china painting class, Heather Harding was suddenly hit with the thought of making a group quilt as a gift to celebrate her mother's eightieth birthday. 'Of course I had never made a quilt before and knew nothing about quiltmaking. I borrowed Jinny Beyer's *Patchwork Patterns*, draughted up thirty blocks and made up thirty fabric packs. These I sent off to all my female relatives. I put the completed blocks together and the quilt was ready in time for her 79th birthday.' Making this quilt fired Heather's imagination and seeing beginners classes advertised a short time later, she was quick to sign up. According to her husband, quiltmaking has since become her obsession. 'Cabin Roses' is from a pattern in a *Quiltmaker* magazine. The original quilt was 165cm square and Heather used graph paper to 'miniaturise the pattern'. The smallness of some pieces created problems and Heather found she had to use a seminole technique when the fabric became too difficult to handle. Heather is pleased with the balance of colour and design the pattern affords and is happy with her completed quilt. She frequently attends specialist workshops, citing tips on easy, efficient methods and techniques as most valuable. 'I don't take the whole quiltmaking thing terribly seriously. I thoroughly enjoy it. The more relaxed I am about what I do, the better it works. Also I have met a super bunch of people. Quilting brings out the niceness in people.'

BLUE MOLA

Christine Henesy
Auckland

115cm by 47cm

Cotton fabrics, ric-rac braid,
stranded thread, needled polyester
batting, reverse-applique.

Christine Henesy recalled that as a child, fabric was what was available. 'My aunt lived with us. She taught me to sew. She was forward-looking and encouraged me to be adventurous with colour.' An 'inveterate class attender', Christine sat School Certificate Art the first year School Certificate was introduced to New Zealand. She said if that made her seem old, she recently met her Art teacher again. This rather elderly lady is still 'creating'. 'I have been interested in all handcrafts and arts available, including needlework, dressmaking and millinery. I am particularly interested in combining patchwork with fashion. I do patchwork and quilting because I cannot not do it. I like to use the fabrics I have on hand. It is much easier to purchase matching fabrics but I enjoy the challenge and feel my work is more interesting and creative by using what I already have.' 'Blue Mola' was inspired by a book Christine was loaned while on a live-in quiltmaking weekend. The book incorporated exercises, as well as a more advanced section on patternmaking. The book was returned at the end of the weekend and Christine carried the ideas home in her head. 'I chose a geranium leaf, the most simple leaf I could find. That was the start of my quilt. I was really doing a series of exercises; I liked the pieces and decided to put them together in a quilt.' Quiltmaking began for Christine in 1982. Classes run by Bonnie Kennedy Grant provided the impetus to continue. 'I appreciate what Bonnie taught me and I appreciate her friendship.'

Polly Lind says she had a rocky start to the art of quiltmaking. Self-taught from American books, she says, 'I started by making a Shoo Fly quilt. The book said to use muslin so I used just that. At that stage I did not know that Americans call muslin what we call calico! After attending a series of beginners classes, I began to do things a bit better but I am still not good at following rules. Inspiration for my wallhanging "At the Quilt Show" just arrived, though no doubt it was associated with the prospect of the Enzed Sewing National Quiltmaking Competition. I did it to put all the miniatures together – it was a fun sort of thing to do. It was meant to look like a quilt show. The idea that not everything in an exhibition is perfect appeals to me and I followed this through.' Polly discarded several pieces, feeling they looked too contemporary. The central block was hand-pieced over papers, while all others were machine-pieced. Polly does not know why she continues to make quilts and feels she just got caught up in the art. 'I worked as a psychiatrist until I retired and I still do not understand why I do it. I will be seventy next year and I am currently having a sewing room added to my house. I have an enormous pile of fabrics. Buying fabrics is really quite irrational. Instead of going out to buy chocolates, I purchase fabrics. As for hand-quilting and all those tiny stitches – I was never going to do that!' Polly feels she has grown in her art over the past few years. She is very keen on dyeing and colour, and plans to work on more contemporary wall projects in the near future.

P rue Martens is fascinated by the lifestyle of the Amish, and working on Amish-inspired projects is her first love. She particularly enjoys the colours dominant in Amish quilts, 'the dark tones and colours and the bold statements these make'. 'Amish Sampler' was constructed from a pattern advertised in an American quiltmaking magazine. Quilting for Prue began five years ago, while living in South Auckland. 'My girlfriend convinced me to attend a series of patchwork and quilting lessons. She was much keener than me. I saw it as a means of getting out of the house one night a week. I didn't do very much to begin with. A year later we moved north and with a change in lifestyle I found time to finish the two sampler quilts I started in class. Soon after, I joined the Kerikeri Quilting Club and now find there are not enough hours in the day to make all the quilts I want to. I have caught the bug.' Prue quilts for relaxation and enjoyment and because it is what she likes doing. 'I haven't got the time to let it take over. I normally buy for the project I am working on and am finding my pile of leftovers is growing. I plan to stick with traditional work. I don't think I could design a contemporary quilt and also, traditional pieces are what I like best.'

AMISH SAMPLER

Prue Martens
Kerikeri

137cm square

Cotton fabrics, cotton batting,
machine-pieced, hand-quilted.

OCEAN WAVES

Yvonne McKenna
Palmerston North

125cm square

Cotton fabrics, wool batting,
machine-pieced, hand-quilted.

Seven years ago, Yvonne McKenna was looking for a hobby and replied to an advertisement for beginners patchwork and quilting classes. Although she was unsure of what the subject was really about, she decided she would attend. She was not immediately hooked but rather dabbled in the art for about twelve months. Then she and a friend joined the Rose City Quilters and 'suddenly I caught the bug'. 'My friend and I attended every workshop going. I started by making small projects but now it is mainly large quilts. I have several pieced tops waiting to be quilted and an assortment of other unfinished projects'. The book, *Let's Make Waves* was the basis of a workshop Yvonne attended through her local club. She felt the workshop would be a good learning experience as the technique used was that of the grid method of speed piecing for the construction of 'triangle squares'. The subject also appealed because of her love of the sea. The use of aqua colours is a deliberate desire to use tones of the ocean. She took some time deciding on the quilting design as she felt it necessary to soften the strong geometric lines. Yvonne enjoys investigating the history of quiltmaking. 'I mainly concentrate on traditional patchwork as I love the history. All traditional blocks have a story and I like to think about that when I am sewing them. I enjoy creating with fabric. I look at fabric and wonder what I can do with it, although I normally start with a pattern and then select the fabrics. There is so much to learn. It is such an absorbing hobby – it gets at me and I want to make each project a little more difficult than the one previously.'

Self-taught from books while living in an isolated South Island community, Jean McLean has certainly mastered the art of fine hand-quilting. Inspired by quilts viewed at Beamish, United Kingdom, in 1989, Jean says, 'I have always looked at the best of old quilts with awe. I wanted to try and emulate them. This is my own pattern, but based strictly on the style of the North of England traditional quilts.' The artist pored over books of old quilts looking for ideas for 'Windermere'. Using individual motifs from various quilts, she rearranged them until she felt happy with the design. 'I think Whole Cloth quilts are very beautiful – people look at them and say, "you can't do that today", but you can.' Jean has been quilting for 15 years and has been influenced by many people. In 1989, she received two firsts at 'Quilt UK' – Hand-Quilting and Wholecloth Quilt, for a fullsized bed quilt.

WINDERMERE

Jean McLean
Blenheim

MERIT AWARD

152cm by 125cm

Cotton sateen, polyester batting, hand-quilted.

A rabian Lights' is the most difficult quilt that either Libby Shallard or Judy Hewin have completed. Judy believes 'some other force was involved in this quilt. I found a box which belonged to my father-in-law. The lid featured the design we used. I knew it would translate into our quilt. The day I showed Libby, a parcel of fabrics arrived. These had been ordered months before and they were perfect for the project.' The quiltmakers worked together on every stage of the quilt. They designed each section as they went, laying the completed pieced area on the floor before deciding their next step. Libby says 'I prefer to work that way. I don't follow a set path. I do it differently every time. Also quilts dictate what they need. Planning from the beginning does not allow for this.' All the decisions in the planning and execution of the quilt were joint. They feel the project was beset with problems from the very beginning. 'For every stitch we sewed, we unpicked two. It would never have been finished if I had had to make it by myself,' said Judy. Quilting posed even more difficulties. Gold thread was used to quilt, as the makers felt the top needed the sparkling effect. The thread required was not available in New Zealand and had to be acquired in Australia. When it arrived it was discovered that the quality was very different to that previously used and it was impossible to quilt with. Once the quilt was completed Judy and Libby felt, for the first time, satisfied with their creation. They have worked on joint projects in the past but this was their most intensive. Judy says, 'You can only work together if you are compatible in your work style as well as your personality.' Libby continued, 'We are lucky. We can bounce ideas off each other. We can pick them up and expand them or conversely, drop them. It is very nice to have company, especially at the quilting stage.'

ARABIAN LIGHTS

Libby Shallard and Judy Hewin
Auckland

WINNER

TRADITIONAL
WALL QUILT

137cm by 195cm

Cotton fabrics, gold lurex (knit and woven), chintz, 80/20 cotton batting, machine-pieced, hand-quilted, trapunto, bead work.

Ann Packer
Wellington

21cm by 17cm

Cotton Liberty lawn, English
batting, paper-pieced,
hand-quilted.

Quiltmaking to Ann Packer 'is my personal creative outlet; it is like a therapy. I like the feeling that I am one of a long line of women stitchers'. Beginning 10 years ago, Ann has worked on a variety of projects both large and small. A special love is making miniature quilts. 'Merlin Sampson started me off on little quilts at the 1984 Symposium. I enjoy making traditional simple patterns that would not work in larger quilts. "Taking Liberties" is the second in a series. The first I made was a gift for a friend whose mother had died. I don't plan my quilts. I feel they are "organic" – that is, they develop over time. I work as a Community Arts Officer which is high-powered and quite chaotic. I think that is why I like to make reasonably tidy quilts.' Ann says she always has something on the go but tends to work in the more traditional. She found she anguished over two contemporary wall quilts she had designed and appreciated the advice of Malcolm Harrison who told her to 'forget it – do what you do well'. Ann particularly enjoys traditional scrap quilts but says, 'It's the fabric that turns me on, especially the pieces with unusual colours. Fabric is what starts me off. I decide on the pattern after I find the fabric.' The friendships that Ann has formed through her interest in quiltmaking are of great importance. 'It's a shared passion. I have two good friends who I rarely see. When we meet, we quilt together. It is a link across cultures and the most wonderful way to make friends.'

'This traditional quilt design, although made with very contemporary fabrics and techniques, still gives the feeling that it has been around for some time. While not trying to imitate the look of a handmade quilt, I was happy to have the chance to demonstrate that a completely machine-made quilt has accuracy and a beauty all of its own. I was inspired by all the beautiful red, orange and magenta fabrics sitting on my shelf. I love the way the mind blends all those seemingly unrelated fabrics into a unified impression of colour and pattern.' Sue Spigel, an American, has lived in New Zealand for the past nine years. For eight of those years, she had been making and selling quilts, clothing and other patchwork items. She started by replying to an advertisement for stall holders for an upcoming craft show. 'I then had to produce the goods. I made lots of small novelties in strip-piecing. I did not sell much but my stall created a lot of interest. I decided to advertise as a teacher. In a day and a half I received 87 replies. I have been quiltmaking ever since.' Sue teaches throughout New Zealand, specialising in the use of border prints in quiltmaking. She recently formed a partnership with two others and has opened a gallery in a Christchurch suburb.

TOMATO PUDDING

Sue Spigel
Christchurch

MERIT AWARD

130cm square

Cotton fabrics, needled polyester batting, machine-pieced, machine-quilted.

'The pattern is traditional. The setting and colours I developed from an Amish crib quilt in the book, *Crib Quilts and other Small Wonders,* by Thomas K. Woodard and Blanche Greenstein. The quilt is reversible. The front is quiet and serene with a soft glow of light, the reverse is strong and vibrant – a mixture of qualities which seem to give the quilt a wholeness of its own.' On completion of 'Autumn Lilies', Gwen was very pleased. 'I love old quilts and was as thrilled with the back as the front.' Gwen says, 'I have treasured handmade textiles from when I was very young. When in the United Kingdom in the early seventies, I haunted museums looking at textiles and old quilts. My grandmother also had a strong interest in textiles; she embroidered, painted and was a woodturner.' Self-taught from books, Gwen feels she works best on her own. She spends a few hours each day working at her sewing machine and hand-quilts most evenings.

AUTUMN LILIES

Gwen Wanigasekera
Hamilton

MERIT AWARD

147cm square

Machine-pieced, hand-quilted, cotton fabrics, cotton chintz, 80/20 cotton batting.

Detail is over the page.

The reverse of 'Autumn Lilies'.

CONTEMPORARY
BED QUILTS

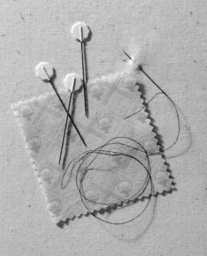

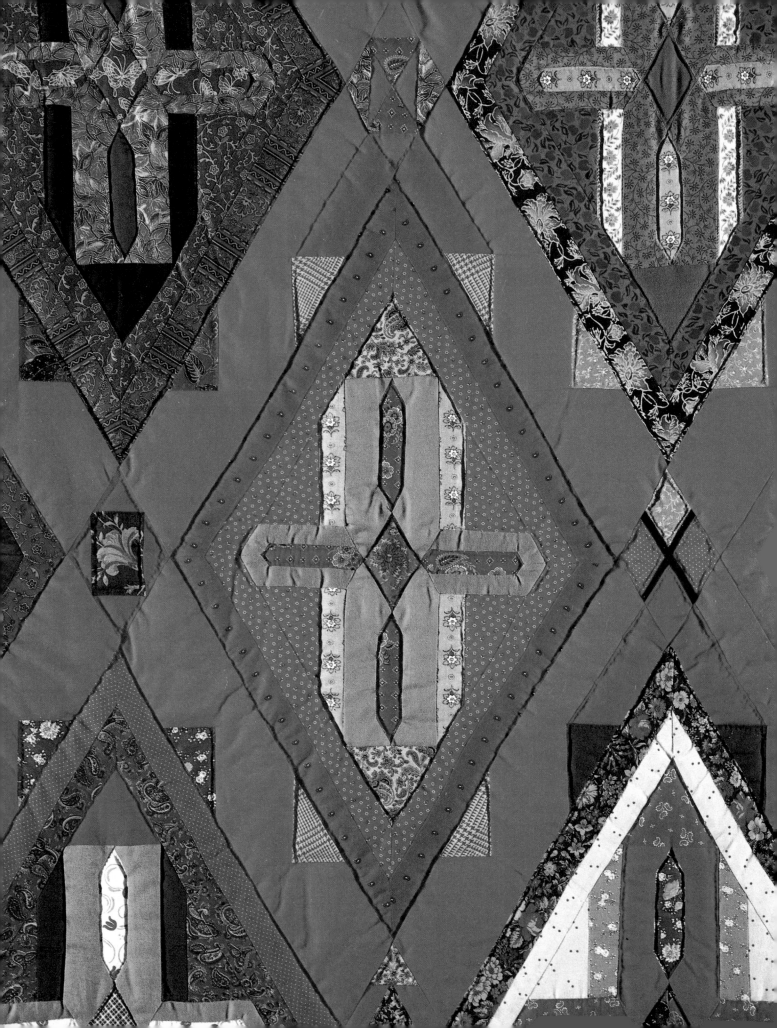

This rather large bed quilt has been made for American friends of Marie Ballagh. A joint project by friends Marie and Rosanne, there were times during the construction of the quilt that they felt the logistics of such a huge project were beyond just one person. Marie says, 'I tend to like variations of traditional quilts. A book of Persian Carpets provided the inspiration for the quilt. The repeating diamond shape has been severely adapted from the original carpet design that so inspired us. It is a loose interpretation.' Although Marie provided the fabric selection, the project was at all times a joint concern. The original design concept called for a central area of repeating diamond shapes with wide strong borders. Initial block designs were constructed and discarded until the right formula was struck. Rosanne baulked at Marie's first prototype block, as it was only six inches long. The block was graphed up to size and work began. The desire for a strength and richness in colour scheme required the use of many like shades of the same base tones. After several blocks were completed, the quiltmakers auditioned various layouts and when satisfied, constructed pieces to fill in the gaps. The border provided a few headaches, one of which features on the reverse of the quilt. Marie says, 'We wanted to play with seminole. Our first designs were too elaborate so it was try, try again. We had a sketchy plan for the whole quilt but we found that most details developed as we worked.' Both women found working together to be a most satisfying experience and would be keen to work on future joint projects. Rosanne says, 'Quilting can be a lonely business. I enjoyed working with Marie and sharing ideas; the give and take. I would certainly consider making other quilts with her.'

RUBY ENCHANTMENT

Marie Ballagh and
Rosanne Anderson
Dunedin

MERIT AWARD

272cm square

Cotton fabrics, lofted polyester batting, machine-pieced, hand-quilted.

A L I Q U O T

Gaylene Bullock
Te Kauwhata

210cm square

Cotton fabrics, wool batting,
machine-pieced, hand-quilted.

A little over two years ago, Gaylene Bullock attended a quilt exhibition and was overcome by what she viewed. 'I found a book on Log Cabin quilts and decided I would make one. A little later I attended a sampler quilt class and learnt to do it properly. Before I discovered quiltmaking, I had tried spinning and weaving and other crafts. None of these left me feeling completely satisfied. Quiltmaking does; it is something I will always do.' Gaylene's desire to make a multi-fabric quilt with a three-dimensional element in print fabrics resulted in 'Aliquot'. She used a method described in *Patchwork Portfolio* to create her pattern. After choosing a design she liked, Gaylene enlarged the pattern to full size. She then divided each piece into equal sizes, and from these cut her templates. 'Because of stretching, I had to be careful with the bias and straights of the diamond shapes. I made the quilt section by section for this reason. I would cut all my fabrics for a whole block, piece these together, and pin it on the wall before starting the next. I quilted the project on a floor frame. This made the process much faster and I find it has improved my quilting.' Gaylene has three special loves in the quilting field. The solid bold bright colours used by the Amish particularly delight her, as do the contrasting prints and colours used by Jinny Beyer. Her other area of interest is in three-dimensional designs, something she hopes to investigate thoroughly. 'I really like innovative pieced work more than I like traditional or contemporary pieces. I like to create something different with a basic block.'

'Italian Zebra' was made by Nan Gardner at the request of her brother. 'He lives in Milan and works in the fashion industry. He has a jetsetting lifestyle, and lives in a trendy chrome and black leather loft apartment. He wanted a black and white quilt. I thought it would never work, I did not think I could please him. I thought about the quilt for two years before finally deciding it was now or never. Fortunately I found a wonderful piece of Liberty chintz in a local emporium. It proved to be a good way of relieving the black and white and adding a splash of colour.' In planning the quilt, Nan deliberately decided to keep the design and technique relatively simple, incorporating strip-quilting, squares and triangles. She chose to do a minimum of hand-quilting, feeling there was enough impact in the piecing. Nan began patchworking more than fifteen years ago, converting her scraps into clothing for her daughters. Three years later she discovered books on the subject of quiltmaking and shortly after joined a group of adventurous women to work on comunally made quilts. Since that time Nan has become obsessed by the art of quiltmaking. 'I have always drawn and I suppose I have a secret passion to be an artist. I feel I am totally indecisive when it comes to a particular style of work. I make both traditional and contemporary quilts – it depends what moves me at the time. I do not think people will ever be able to look at my work and say, "that is a Nan Gardner quilt". I adore fabric shops and am happy just to wander around them. To me they are like an art gallery. It is the fabrics and colours and the need of a creative outlet that keeps me quiltmaking.'

ITALIAN ZEBRA

Nanette Gardner
Auckland

215cm by 190cm

Cottons, polished cottons,
wool batting, machine-pieced,
hand-quilted.

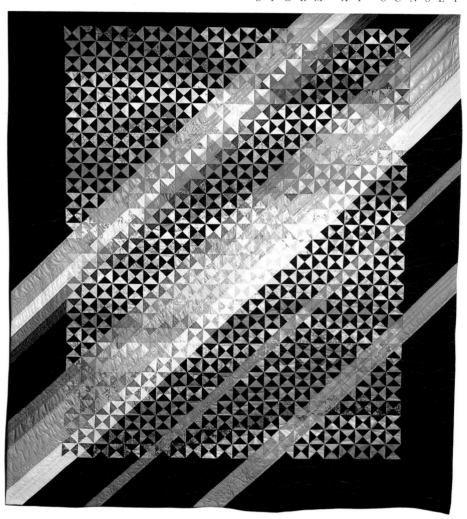

From 1983 to 1985 Marge Hurst studied for a Certificate of Embroidery from the City and Guilds of London. Her first assignment was in patchwork. 'I knew I would like patchwork about 35 years ago! I stayed away from it because I thought it would take over, which it has.' Marge was inspired to make 'Storm at Sunset' by the many sunsets she has viewed from her home and from Pukerua Beach. 'I cannot remember how I began using triangles to contrast background colour. I usually have colours I take from nature running through the background. I pinned hundreds of background triangles on my board, in a preplanned layout creating diagonal stripes. Then I chose fabric for the sunset and I arranged these in a colourwash.' The reverse of this quilt is also pieced – the colours represent the fresh colours of the morning after a storm.

STORM AT SUNSET

Marge Hurst
Pukerua Bay

WINNER
CONTEMPORARY
BED QUILT

225cm by 224cm

Machine-pieced, machine-quilted, cottons, cotton blends, silks, furnishing fabrics, wool batting.

Detail is over the page.

'Bright Morning' — the reverse of
'Storm at Sunset'.

'Firelight 2' is the second quilt in a series made by Judy Perreau exploring the differences between hot and cold colours. 'I am interested in the "feeling" and the contrasts when playing with colour, and feel that warmth or coolness can be displayed well this way. I like the Log Cabin block and use it often. I sew my fabrics directly onto batting as I don't like the look of machine-quilting on the quilt top.' Seven years ago, Judy attended beginners patchwork and quilting classes. At the class she met a like-minded person and the two formed a partnership to open a quiltmaking supplies shop in Christchurch. For several years Judy tutored in beginners techniques, something she was happy to give up. More recently she and a silk painter have joined forces and opened Designer Gallery in Christchurch central, where she sells many of the items she produces. Judy also designs a range of pieced toilet and cosmetic bags which she markets throughout the South and lower North Islands. She travels New Zealand selling her own patchwork products at the annual Craft Affairs. Judy says, 'I think I am a frustrated painter. Fabric is a medium I can use for my creative skills but as a quiltmaker, I feel I'm only just beginning.' Judy says, she has a 'minimal fabric collection'. 'I am very fussy about what I buy. If I like it I buy it – the cost doesn't concern me.'

FIRELIGHT 2

Judy Perreau
Christchurch

245cm by 150cm

Silks, cottons, lurex, other assorted textured fabrics, needled polyester batting, machine-pieced, 'quilt-as-you-go'.

'I could see this quilt in my mind and I wanted to make it – I had to make it.' In 1989, Gwen Wanigasekera made several wall hangings derived from the Pineapple Log Cabin pattern, and the wish to explore the technique further inspired her to make this quilt. 'The quilt was developed from a small sketch I made. I then translated one quarter of the pattern onto graph paper. I transposed the design onto vilene and sewed the fabrics, in reverse, on this pattern. It was necessary for me to hand-dye silk, as many of the shades of colours I required were not available. I intended this quilt to fit on the top of a King or Queen-sized bed with a black spread underneath and black pillowslips.' The quilt was made in four sections and put together after machine-quilting was completed. 'I was very pleased with the quilt when it was finished. New patterns emerged which I hadn't expected. I thought the grid design would disappear but it didn't entirely. The quilt expressed what I wanted it to. Ancient civilisations worshipped the sun, the moon, the earth, but we have forgotten these things. We have to treasure them.' It took Gwen over two months of constant work to make 'Putanga O Te Ra'. Two of the more tedious jobs were frequently changing the thread for machine-quilting and sewing in all thread ends. Her love of Log Cabin means she plans to work in this area for at least the next year.

PUTANGA O TE RA
(BIRTH OF THE SUN)

Gwen Wanigasekera
Hamilton

QUILT OF THE SHOW

176cm square

Cottons, cotton blends, chintz, satins, percentage-dyed silks, 80/20 cotton batting, machine-pieced, machine-quilted.

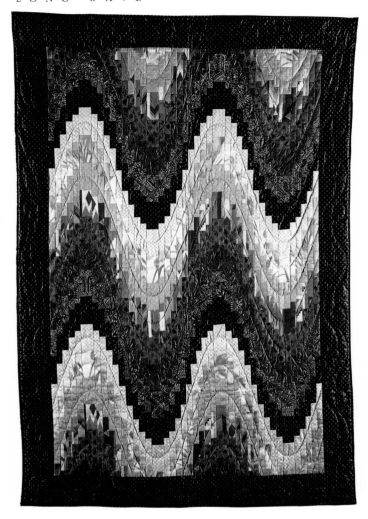

LONG WAVE

Elizabeth Suter
Waikanae Beach

203cm by 135cm

Cotton furnishing fabrics, wool
batting, machine strip-pieced,
hand-quilted.

Eighteen months ago, Elizabeth Suter joined the Pinestream Patchwork and Quilters group to learn how to make quilts, something which had interested her since childhood. This is her first completed bed quilt. 'I found this quilt a real challenge. I was inspired to make the quilt after reading a strip-piecing book by Diane Wold, and through my love of mathematics. I am a mathematics teacher. I love the geometry of patchwork and I enjoy doing things with my hands. I have always liked craftwork.' After sorting through her vast collection of fabrics, Elizabeth selected and laid out her choices. These she auditioned for a few weeks, occasionally changing some colours. She says, 'Every bit of making the quilt was pleasure. It was much better than I expected. I was delighted with the finished quilt and the result was a nice surprise. The quilt reflects my love of the beach. The colours suggest the different types of driftwood and shells left after a storm, and the wave pattern – the sea. The Maori quilting design on the border is called "ngaru-roa", meaning long wave and this seemed particularly appropriate for 1990.' Elizabeth certainly does not intend this to be her last quilt. 'I'm busy experimenting with all techniques. I like working with fabric, especially furnishing fabrics. I like the softer colours and the greater variety. I have a number of boxes of older curtain samples – really it is a vast collection. I think that I will work more on wall hangings, contemporary ones.'

CONTEMPORARY
WALL QUILTS

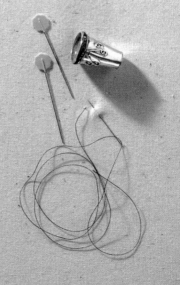

Catherine says she has thirteen years' experience as an amateur quiltmaker and two years' experience as a serious amateur. Two years ago, she joined two fellow quilters with the aim of making more artistic quilts and wall pieces. Six weeks after entering the Enzed Sewing National Quiltmaking Competition, Catherine attended her first class in the art form, a machine-quilting class. Inspiration for the quilt came from the thought that 'the forming of a quilt is similar to that of a flower blooming; it opens in stages until it is a complete bloom'. She says, 'I see this quilt in three stages of birth – first, the black pod is opening to show the shards of mingled colour beyond. The second stage has the pod frills folding back to reveal the shards on the inside, but at a further stage of pattern development, although not yet able to be seen fully. Finally, the quilt is "out" – the true pattern has emerged. All the shards fit into place. In the corner a new quilt is beginning to burst through and the whole process will be repeated.' Catherine thought about the project for six months before construction began. The first and third pieces in the series were completed before the second, and most difficult, was tackled. 'I spent a lot of time working on the fabric folds to make them perfect. Sometimes a quilt doesn't work – this one did.' Catherine is keen to continue working on three-dimensional projects and also to dye and paint her own fabrics.

BIRTH OF A QUILT SERIES — EVOLVE

Catherine Bell
Christchurch

MERIT AWARD

55cm by 40cm (three pieces)

Cottons, cotton blends, cotton chintz, machine-pieced, machine and hand-quilted, polyester batting and fibre fill.

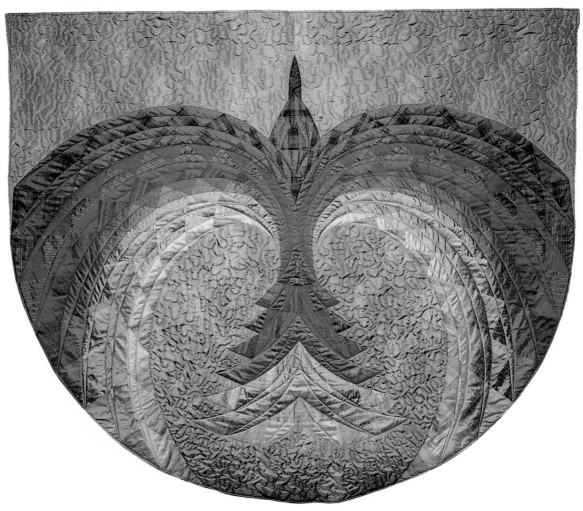

MIGRATION

Barbara Bilyard
Auckland

WINNER

CONTEMPORARY
WALL QUILT

178cm by 195cm

Machine-pieced, machine-quilted,
silks, polyester taffeta,
polyester batting.

Seven days prior to the deadline for all entries in the Enzed Sewing National Quiltmaking Competition, only one half of this quilt was pieced. Barbara was unsure if she could complete the quilt in time, but the belief that she does her best work under pressure encouraged her to continue. Having spent some time working on a quilt made to commemorate the 1990 Commonwealth Games held in Auckland, and reading articles on the recent influx of Asian immigrants to New Zealand, Barbara felt inspired to make a quilt celebrating the ongoing migration of peoples to, and within, the Pacific region. She chose the traditional Flying Geese pattern as the basis of her design. 'I haven't wanted to break free from the heritage of geometric patterns. The Flying Geese used to piece the wings of the bird represent the continuing migration to and within the Pacific. I feel all people add colour and richness to our society.' The quilt spent some time in the design stage before work began on piecing. A large scale drawing was made and Barbara cleverly managed to make each wing and each tail segment identical, therefore only one set of templates were required for each. 'I wanted to make a circular quilt but I compromised the shape for easier hanging.' Barbara began quiltmaking seven years ago, making a quilt for her youngest child. So enthralled with quiltmaking, she made enough blocks for three quilts. 'After dabbling in many crafts, I knew this one was the one I was searching for.' Barbara has had one solo and two joint exhibitions, and is a past President of the Auckland Patchworkers and Quilters Guild. She belongs to two Auckland groups – the Sew and Sews and the P's and Q's. Teaching several specialist workshops in contemporary quiltmaking, colour and design, takes her around New Zealand.

The quiltmaker was inspired to make this quilt when she discovered the pattern Good Morning Glory in a *Quiltmaker*. She felt this pattern lent itself to colour exploration, an area in which she was keen to experiment. The quilt took a lot of planning, and fabric collection took some time. The effect Jane desired was of colour movement – from dark to light with sparkle and highlights. Although she initially saw her design as the night sky, Jane soon realised the work reminded her of the ripples created on a pool when a pebble is dropped in. From the beginning, she wanted to quilt her project in circles to enhance the movement present. She says, 'The wallhanging shows the sparkling highlights on the water moving through to the deepening shadows on the outer edge of the pool.' Jane spent many hours quilting with special friends to complete this project. She recalls shared meals and quilting into the small hours, the comradeship, and the inspiration from other quilters. The artist has been quiltmaking for ten years and has made about twelve large projects and innumerable smaller ones. She frequently travels in the course of her work and always carries hand-piecing with her, often in the form of miniatures, of which she is a fan.

DEEP POOLS

Jane Boyd
Auckland

MERIT AWARD

170cm square

Cotton fabrics, polished cottons, reversed fabrics, 80/20 cotton batting, machine-pieced, hand-quilted.

SUMMER FANTASY

Vonda Clarke
Hamilton

70cm by 86cm

Cottons, cotton blends,
machine-pieced, hand-quilted,
needled polyester batting.

'I saw a photograph of a quilt made by Susan Denton and wanted to try her technique in an original design of my own. We holiday each year at Whangamata. This quilt reminds me of there – the channel from the harbour, the open sea, the sandy beaches and the pine forest.' In making 'Summer Fantasy', Vonda says she tried to put her ideas on paper, but was not sure what she was making until she started putting the project together. 'I could see Whangamata begin to form. I would have liked to make the quilt bigger but I ran out of material. The quilting controlled itself. I knew I wanted the sea to look like sea. Stipple quilting the sand was a last minute decision. I'm pleased – the quilt really needed it.'

Sandra Cunningham never intended to become a quiltmaker. She had no history of stitchery but working part-time for a quilt teacher stimulated her to try the art. Even then she had no idea how absorbed she would become. After making a few traditional quilts, Sandra realised that it was contemporary quilts, particularly pictorial quilts, that interested her most. A book of twenties Vogue covers provided the inspiration for this quilt. 'The picture was of the figures only. I really liked the strong bold colours and the straight lines of the people. I wanted the challenge of interpreting this picture in fabric and creating an appropriate background.' The original picture was enlarged by photocopier machine and then Sandra sectioned the enlargement and drew a plan on graph paper. The background 'popped into her mind'. 'I chose to create the illusion of night time and of being outdoors. The colours needed to blend with the atmosphere I planned to create.' Six months of fairly intensive work was involved in the making of this quilt. Sandra says of her quilt, 'I connect my quilt with an era; I am very interested in the early 1900s. I think of this period as magical, mystical and carefree. This is what these figures are to me. They have no obvious faces, all is behind the masks. They remind me of women who dress up to create an image as a means of escape.' Sandra has been quiltmaking for nearly four years and is not certain what her next project will be, although she is keen to continue working in a similar vein.

VENETIAN NIGHTS

Sandra Cunningham
Napier

195cm by 240cm

Cottons, polycotton moiree, polyester batting, hand-pieced, hand-appliqued, hand-quilted.

BLUES GARDEN

Valerie Cuthbert
Auckland

126cm by 80cm

Machine-pieced, hand-quilted,
hand-dyed and painted cottons,
cotton blends, Italian lace and
brocade, needled polyester batting.

Inspiration for 'Blues Garden' came from a sixteenth-century traditional Japanese strip-piecing method Valerie used for several years in kimono construction. She says 'It lends itself to random Log Cabin construction, and in turn suggests flower shapes or butterflies. The fabrics helped inspire the design.' Valerie began quiltmaking in 1980 after viewing the quilts of a local artist. 'It knocked me off my feet. I looked up a dictionary to check the meaning of "patchwork" and "quilting". I pored over old *McCall* magazines and then just started. I couldn't follow a pattern. In fact, I don't want to follow a pattern.' She has sold, exhibited and taught quiltmaking since 1983, both here and in Australia. A member of the Academy of Fine Arts, Valerie also belongs to the Auckland Co-operative, Elephant House. She considers herself a contemporary quiltmaker not bound by the restraints of traditional teachings. In making 'Blues Garden', the artist chose a wide variety of fabrics, largely hand-dyed and painted cottons, polyester cottons, Italian lace and brocade, to give a variety of surface textures. Some pieces have been marbled. There are also some shibori pieces. The quilt is made up of freely sewn Log Cabin blocks joined by six strips and hand-quilted in a variety of coloured threads, including metallic, in free flowing lines and swirls. The quilt is bagged out and tied. Valerie wanted to show contrasts between light and dark, vivid colours and pastels, curves and rectangles. She says, 'It can be seen as a garden; upside down it becomes the night sky. I like it either way.'

Brenda Dapson has been quiltmaking for the past nine years but says, 'I am just getting started – I'm still doing my apprenticeship.' Brenda attended a local drop-in centre when her children were quite small and eventually followed the centre tutor to night classes she was running. For three years, Brenda was content to learn techniques in patchwork, quilting and embroidery but the wish to explore more contemporary areas initiated her decision to move away from traditional. Brenda still occasionally attends classes with her original tutor to learn a new technique or to have contact with others. Her first contemporary piece was a Kaleido-scope quilt. 'I mainly go for colour and illusion. I like light and dark. Michael James and Nancy Halpern, two American quiltmakers, have been a positive influence on me.' Inspired to make 'Environmental Harmony' by 'a thing I have about trees', she wanted to do something to look up to. Brenda can see an end product before beginning a quilt. 'I don't draw; the quilt does what it wants to.' She spent two days English piecing the batik background. On to this she appliqued the tree. From there it was three months of intense work to stab-stitch quilt and embroider the project. 'I want to do another tree quilt; I am never satisfied with the work I do. The magic for me is what fabric does, how it changes and how it does what it wants. When you cut it down, it does something totally different to what you expect.'

ENVIRONMENTAL
HARMONY

Brenda Dapson
Taradale

158cm by 68cm

Cottons, silk batiks, leather,
polyester batting, paper-piecing,
hand-appliqued,
hand-embroidered, hand-quilted.

Rita Easther
Feilding

MERIT AWARD

122cm × 80cm

Cotton fabrics, hand-dyed cottons,
needled polyester batting,
hand-pieced, hand and
machine-appliqued,
machine-quilted.

Rita Easther was a painter of some renown 'but because it became bigger than me I shut the door on it'. Later she met Pitt Henrich a professional Fabric Artist from Auckland and was greatly inspired by her. 'My greatest love is expressing my own ideas. I have made a number of church banners which satisfy my need to express my faith.' Rita was inspired to create 'Lamentations: A Mother's Story' by her feeling of sadness as her children left home – some to settle permanently overseas. The artist drew a small detailed sketch which she then painted and finally enlarged to full scale. She felt unhappy with the finished quilt, feeling that she had rushed to finish it. She would have liked to work more slowly and to have had hand-dyed silks especially for the project. Rita says, 'The quilt shows a mother bird's surprise and sadness at the empty nest. Three little ones are flying off happily and the other two birds have come to grief – one has a broken wing and the other has died.' Quiltmaking is not Rita's greatest love, but she plans to continue working in the art because of the fellowship. When asked why she works in fabrics, Rita said, 'Painting is so messy, fabric is clean and you can try a piece. It's not the same with paint. A mistake becomes a catastrophe. You can't just paint it out. I paint with my needle.'

HIGHRISE SUNSET

Mary Fletcher
Dunedin

135cm square

Machine-pieced, machine-quilted,
cotton fabrics, cotton blends,
needled polyester batting.

Mary, a quiltmaker of ten years, has only recently turned to designing her own quilts. Her desire to experiment with colour-shading to obtain a three-dimensional effect was the major inspiration for this quilt. She also wished to incorporate highrise buildings within her design. Mary based her quilt on the block 'Boxed Star' by Jinny Beyer. She fragmented the block and shaded the many small pieces. While trying to get the colours as the wanted them, Mary became most frustrated. The yellow and orange segments of the quilt were not going according to plan, with the result that the pieces were thrown in the rubbish bin. Fortunately, they were retrieved by her daughter and the quilt was completed. Mary says of her quilt, 'I see in this quilt four highrise towers meeting at a central point, the triangular pieces between the towers giving the effect of looking down from a height to the ground below. Being on the same side, the red, orange and yellow segment gives the impression of the sun setting in the west.' A background as a home-sewer encouraged Mary to begin her first quilt. She thinks she probably owns the only seven-pointed star in existence. She says, 'I cannot not do patchwork. I love working with fabrics and with colour. I will have to live three or four lifetimes to use up all my fabrics.' Mary is excited by the area in which she is currently working. 'I love three-dimensional work. Katie Pasquini and Jinny Beyer have been a great inspiration to me. I find this area, along with colour and fabric, marries all the things I love doing. I have such feeling for the quilts I make – I want to make a name for myself as a quiltmaker.'

ANNIVERSARY

Liz Gates
Feilding

170cm by 106cm

Machine-pieced, hand-quilted,
hand-appliqued, cotton and
cotton blends, Silver Fern and
wording from a printed panel,
2oz polyester batting.

Last May, Colin Gates received a duvet cover featuring a Silver Fern and the words 'New Zealand All Blacks'. Liz, his wife, fearful that the duvet would be given pride of place on the lounge wall, decided she would convert it into a quilt. She says, 'I can see how rugby can intrude into the world of quilting and quilting into the world of rugby. I made this quilt to show the loves of two people – my husband's love of rugby and my love of quilting. It is to celebrate our 20th wedding anniversary.' Liz used a rugby encyclopaedia to name and date all of New Zealand's twenty-seven present Rugby Union provinces. The same book provided Liz with correct provincial colours. Piecing began last August and when completed, Liz chose to lap-quilt the project for portability. She was delighted with the interest the quilt provoked. Men especially were full of questions. Several coincidences occurred while the work was in progress. The jersey quilted on New Year's Day was that of a century old rugby club, the double anniversary of the Gates' and New Zealand's Sesqui Centennial; local judging for the competition occurred the day before the Gates' wedding anniversary and Liz was unable to present her husband with the quilt. Liz says, 'I love any kind of handcraft and have always sewn. I enjoy working with lovely fabrics and playing with colour. I try many different techniques and cannot stick to the rules. I enjoy making more contemporary quilts but using traditional method.'

As a child, Pat Gibson felt overwhelmed by the talents and abilities of her siblings and believed she lacked any artistic or creative potential. 'I was the practical one. My sisters both died at a young age. I thought they were so clever, I felt I had to do something for them.' In 1985, inspired by an exhibition at the Academy of Fine Arts, Pat decided to 'paint pictures with fabric'. Since that time, she has exhibited at the Academy each year and was granted Artist Membership in 1987. A 1949 photograph of her mother and a friend inspired Pat to make this quilt. 'It was a combination of my interest in fabric portraits and the desire to put visible sunshine into my work. I am impressed by quilts which use lights and darks to create sunshine and shadow.' Pat used the grid method to enlarge the postcard-sized photograph and 'grabbed any fabric she thought was the right texture or colour'. 'I pinned these on a board I have on my balcony and auditioned them from the bottom of my garden. Once the selection was made, I first did the applique, pieced the background and then to that applied the people. I made the quilt in a week. I found it a great pleasure to do – working long hours – sometimes I even forgot to eat.' Pat is pleased with the finished product. She says of 'Life is a Patchwork of Memories', 'It is a quilt capturing a moment in time of the days of hats and gloves, a sunny day, a chat, and memories to share. Patchwork using fabrics speaks of past times.' Pat says 'When I see something beautiful I want to capture it another way, in fabric or in paint. Quiltmaking fills a big gap in my life and is extremely necessary. I also have masses of fabrics I have to use before I die.'

LIFE IS A PATCHWORK OF MEMORIES

Pat Gibson
Wainuiomata

83cm by 68cm

Cotton fabrics, needled polyester batting, machine-pieced, machine-appliqued, machine-quilted.

VILLAGE VISTA

Jeanette Gillies
Wanaka

200cm × 150cm

Machine and hand-pieced,
hand-quilted, 100% cotton fabrics,
80/20 cotton batting.

Jeanette, a quilter for ten years, has completed ten quilts although she says this was the most difficult. She was requested to photograph buildings and other repeating shapes for an advanced Seminole Class she attended at Symposium '89. She had a vision of houses disappearing into the distance and wondered, if through seminole, she could achieve this. Finding she could not, she immediately joined her 'graph-plate' together and, with perspective help from her daughter, she began to design her quilt. Firstly she drew in the main vertical lines to achieve a vanishing point and perspective, and then designed suitable houses to fit the spaces. She says, 'I kept the design as simple as possible and used colour-fading for the disappearing effect. I added homely touches of trees, gardens, a quilt airing on a verandah, "lace" wrought iron work, a light left on, fences, a letterbox and a cat to convey a sense of family spirit. The warm terracotta-coloured roof was deliberately chosen in the hope viewers could relate to memories of a happy home.' The archway proved difficult as it took Jeanette some time to find a suitable fabric. Stipple quilting was a breakthrough for Jeanette as she found she could achieve a suitable texture for the grass. Many different shades of thread were used for quilting achieved by the 'stab-stitch' method. On completion of the quilt, the artist asked her husband his opinion, saying 'there's a lot of work in it'. His comment was, 'Yes, all that gardening'.

FLIGHTS OF FANTASY

Margaret Groen and
Renee Campbell
Napier

180cm by 120cm

Cottons, hand-dyed cottons,
polycottons, satin, machine-pieced,
hand-quilted, hand-appliqued,
polyester batting.

Margaret introduced Renee, her friend of thirty years, to patchwork in 1988. Margaret at that stage had been quiltmaking for three years, doing a variety of traditional and more innovative projects. They always knew they would make a quilt together and, says Margaret, 'The exhibition was the catalyst. I found a picture on the cover of a School Publications Catalogue, and I said to Renee, "This is the quilt we are going to make." She agreed and I set about drawing up a full-sized plan. We then cut it up and used it as templates. We had to number everything carefully; the balloons have many pieces – in fact, the large balloon has over 150 pieces.' As Margaret cut, Renee sewed. The balloons took five days to complete but as the ladies both work, they could only spare one day a week each. Renee also appliqued the balloons onto the background fabric. 'She is the expert sewer,' said Margaret. Margaret was responsible for hand-quilting. Both ladies were surprised at how easy the quilt was to construct and the speed at which they were able to work. Both would recommend joint projects.

This is the first quilt Pauline Hunt, a quiltmaker since 1971, has made after a break of five years. She had spent that time 'thinking about what quiltmaking means to me'. 'I have always looked at things in terms of quiltmaking. I like the social aspect of materials and how they reflect the fashions of the times.' Pauline, who works full-time as an artist, has worked in fabric for as long as she can remember, enjoying the feel, the colours and the sociability of the medium. She says she is a 'lousy' sewer, but that does not restrict her from using patchwork techniques in an individual and creative way. 'Family Tree' features an old family photograph, that of her grandparents' wedding. Pauline made a high contrast bromide, and then a photographic silk screen to transfer the image onto fabric. The photograph was then surrounded by lace which Pauline had coloured with gilt pen. Various embellishments were added, including organza, tulle and embroidery. 'I like layers. My ideas changed as the quilt progressed and there was also the pressure of time.' The artist originally intended that trees should be visible at the top of the quilt and that roots would feature at the bottom. 'These tended to disappear. The background just grew. I wanted a contemporary version of an old family photograph in a gilt frame, breaking up and disintegrating with time.' Pauline loathed the quilt by the time it was completed. She is only now, three months later, beginning to enjoy it. 'I would like to make "Family Tree" again. This time I would plan more thoroughly and have a clearer idea before I start. I want to incorporate a certain roughness in my quilts, frayed edges and unfinished piecing. I plan to manipulate fabrics.'

FAMILY TREE

Pauline Hunt
Hamilton

170cm by 230cm

Machine and hand-pieced, hand-appliqued, hand-embroidered, cottons, cotton blends, tulle, organza, and other fabrics.

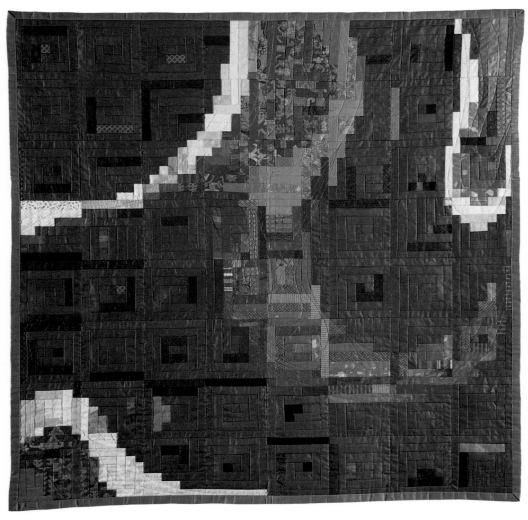

DANCING CORAL

Marge Hurst
Pukerua Bay

99cm square

Machine-pieced, machine-quilted,
cotton, cotton blends, silks,
furnishing fabrics, heavy calico
inner layer.

Marge frequently makes quilts using traditional patchwork shapes in very innovative and contemporary ways. The two quilts she had in the exhibition are two such quilts. 'I want people to see colour as colour, to see how it works together and what happens when the background is changed. With my Log Cabin-based quilts, I started drawing lines then I transposed them onto a Log Cabin grid I had drawn up. I read an article about a Japanese quiltmaker and that was how I got started.'

A family wedding on a Marae encouraged Glenis Jones to consider making a quilt with an ethnic flavour. A short time later while visiting a Wellington market, she found a placemat which formed the basis of her design. Interpreting the design was another matter! Glenis found she needed to spend a long time preparing her fabrics and shapes before stitching could begin. She says, 'I really liked the theme of the quilt, especially this being the year of New Zealand's Sesqui Centennial. I see the white man being superimposed over the black man and they in turn being superimposed over each other. I feel that this is how it should be. We should be living as one people sharing the best of the other's culture. The surrounding fern fronds represent our country and the reverse of the quilt portrays the sea, our lakes and our rivers.' The quilt posed many challenges for Glenis. Having the basic design on the placemat was a useful guide for her. The number of fabric layers provided her with several difficult periods. A workshop run by Malcolm Harrison in reverse machine-applique gave Glenis the confidence to complete her project. Three years ago, a lifelong interest in sewing encouraged Glenis to attend a beginners patchwork and quilting class. Completely hooked, Glenis says, 'I love the challenge of creating. I find there is always something to learn, and everyone has something to offer. I enjoy attending workshops and discovering new techniques. I like to combine a variety of skills from various classes in each quilt I complete.'

KIA ORA AI TE TANGATA (GOOD HEALTH AND LIFE TO ALL MANKIND)

Glenis Jones
Napier

112cm by 91cm

Cotton fabrics, English batting, reverse machine-applique, machine-quilted.

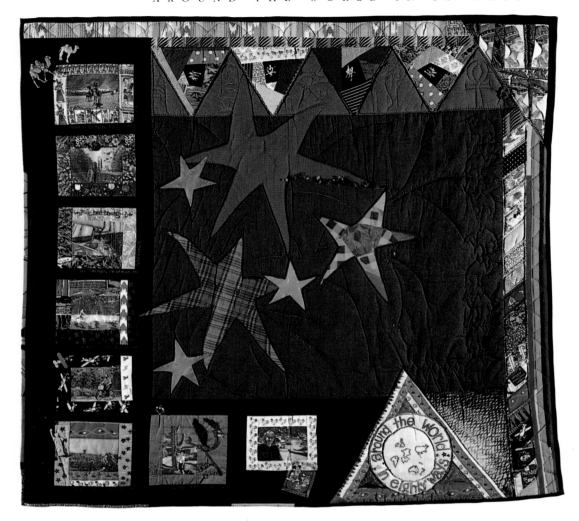

Inspired by an extensive travel itinerary which included Egypt, Europe, North America and the Pacific, Sara Koller constructed this charming momento. The markets of Cairo, Habitat of London – 'the best store in the world', the gutters of the Paris fashion quarter, and Bloomingdales of New York all provided Sara with fabrics for this 'my personal momento of a very important experience'. Faithfully washed and ironed, these pieces were cherished inclusions in her luggage. The artist made various sketches of the proposed quilt as she travelled the world, but found that once construction began the project was not at all as she had envisioned. Photographs taken during her travels were to be transposed onto fabric and these were to feature on her quilt. Unable to procure this service in Australia where she was living at the time, Sara had to send her photographs to the United States. Colouring and embellishing these images took many months in a project that lasted three years. 'It's nice to have the quilt as a constant reminder of the places I visited. I like to collect things and being able to embellish my quilt with them makes my collecting worthwhile.' While working on the quilt, Sara spent three months studying embroidery in Australia with a French tutor. She was encouraged to follow her instincts and not get bogged down with perfection, 'something I had trouble with until then'. Sara has always had a passion for fabric. 'I like to use fabric and beads and sequins in things other than clothing, things I can look at all the time.'

AROUND THE WORLD IN 80 WAYS

Sara Koller
Auckland

142cm by 150cm

Hand and machine-pieced, hand-embroidered, hand-quilted, various fabrics including hand-dyed cottons, silks, assorted embellishments, polyester batting.

EVERYWHERE

Judy LeHeron
Palmerston North

108cm by 70cm

Cottons, cotton blends, lame, satin
ribbon, needled polyester batting,
hand-pieced, hand-quilted.

Self-taught, Judy LeHeron began quiltmaking in 1975. She had always admired quilts and found the progression a natural one from home dressmaking. A family of three and part-time work results in a limited output of what she regards as her lifetime hobby. Her initial work was in the traditional sphere but construction of church banners five or six years ago 'opened my eyes to abstract designs'. The rich colours of stained glass inspired Judy to make 'Everywhere'. 'At first glance I wanted my quilt to represent a stained glass window but in fact it reflects my love of my environment – the earth, the sky, the sea and God's love for all creation. The image is repeated on the reverse of the quilt to complete the impression of seeing through a stained glass window. The quilt also emphasises that "Everywhere" includes places and things we cannot see, just as we cannot see both sides of the quilt at one time.' Judy began working on a quilt nearly four times the size of her completed project. She had problems with the asymmetrical shape of many of the pieces. These being slightly on the bias, stretched and made piecing difficult. She is currently completing the original quilt but says it definitely will not be reversible. The colours were chosen as representative of the bright clear colours of stained glass and black ribbon used to 'lead light' the quilt. For the past eight years, Judy has met weekly with a multi-craft group called The Selfish Sewing Circle. 'Selfish because we are doing it for ourselves. I find the group a good forum for new ideas. I love quiltmaking. I like colours, and I like shapes. The way they come together and the changes that occur when the finished patchwork is quilted intrigues me. I like to paint with fabric.'

Jean has two distinctly diverse styles. 'I like to have a go at different things.' 'Anthena' was inspired by a photograph of a misty scene in the *National Geographic*. Jean simplified the picture to make it workable and then enlarged it. 'I spent a lot of time choosing fabrics and pinning them on the wall. I would leave it for a while and perhaps rearrange them.'

ANTHENA

Jean McLean
Blenheim

95cm by 132cm

Hand-pieced, hand-appliqued, hand-embroidered, machine-quilted, 100% cotton fabrics, polyester batting.

THE EARTH BREAKS
OUT IN PRAISE OF
GOD

Sue McMillan
Christchurch

81cm by 88cm

Machine-pieced, hand-quilted,
cotton fabrics, hand-dyed
cottons, needled dacron batting.

This, the first quilt made by Sue McMillan, was conceived and constructed while she was pregnant, and on bed rest, with her second child. 'I wanted to convey the beauty of God's creation in a spring scene – blossoms above, daffodils underfoot and a willow tree in new leaf. It was also an experiment to see if I could achieve a three-dimensional effect and show light. My creator was my inspiration.' Sue chose Hagley Park, Christchurch, as her subject, took several photographs and, from there, drew a sketch. She then divided the sketch into a grid pattern, modified it slightly and began to reproduce it with fabrics. 'I attached my pieces to a pinboard and would lie back and view it. I spent hours looking at the quilt, and manipulating the pieces. I allowed myself an hour up each day to work on the quilt'. She was surprised by the number of different fabrics she required to complete her quilt. Never having made a quilt before meant she had to purchase fabrics especially for the project. 'I bought about twenty-four small pieces but ended up using about 140 different fabrics.' The artist feels she probably became involved in quiltmaking, because of the influence of her mother, Pat Gibson, a well-known Wellington quiltmaker. Although this is her first quilt, it is certainly not her last. 'I have about eight quilts in my head I am bursting to do. I aim to keep improving, maybe one day to win a national competition.'

Margaret, a Home Science graduate from Otago, feels this quilt is most untypical of her. As a dressmaking tutor and more latterly a quilt teacher, Margaret specialises in machine-work. Her inspiration for the quilt came from the magnificent scenery in and around Queenstown where she lives. She was also inspired by the work of Jinny Beyer and Deidre Amsden, both of whom tutored and lectured at Symposium '89, which Margaret attended. The quilt is a stylised representation of the first glimpse the quiltmaker has of Lake Wakatipu as she drives into Queenstown each day. She says, 'I'm surrounded by majestic mountains, a beautiful lake and a countryside that changes quite distinctly with the seasons. I feel this quilt shows the grandeur and the power of the mountains around us, and the mood of a cool winter's day.' Margaret drew an outline for the quilt on isometric graph paper, worked out her shading and then grouped her fabrics into different values before making her choices. The quilt took eight months to complete, although the last weeks saw Margaret working constantly on the project.

WAKATIPU COUNTRY

Margaret Melhop
Queenstown

125cm by 100cm

Hand-pieced over papers, cotton fabrics, 2oz polyester batting, hand-quilted.

Margaret Morrison
Palmerston North

147cm square

Cottons, cotton blends, polyester,
lofted polyester batting,
machine-pieced, machine-quilted.

Margaret Morrison cites her first patchwork experience on a sewing machine as 'the stitching together of travellers' samples'. 'My mother did patchwork, making clothing and small items for church fairs. I had a marvellous time cutting up the pieces. I always wanted to cut just a few more. It's the fabric that makes me do patchwork. I have always considered that proper patchwork is scrap patchwork. Until about ten years ago, it seemed wrong to me to buy fabrics, but even then I was very selective with what I used. It has to look right.' Ten years ago Margaret, an enthusiastic embroiderer, was invited to teach patchwork and at that stage became involved in quiltmaking. 'Now I can't help but do it. I would feel very frustrated if I couldn't make quilts. My definition of heaven is to be able to complete all the quilts I have not had time to make on this earth.' Margaret planned her quilt on graph paper before choosing fabrics. After trying her colours against white and shades of grey, she decided that they worked best with black. Triangles are the shapes she enjoys working with most. 'I find them fascinating, there is so much one can do with triangles. The interchange of shapes in the block pattern I chose for this quilt, when set side by side, really inspired me. I am fascinated by the way colour associations alter the way we see individual colour and shade, and also by the way these colour associations are present in nature if we look for them. It was after I had chosen the colours and planned the quilt, that I realised that the colours I selected are to be found in zinnias, one of my favourite flowers.'

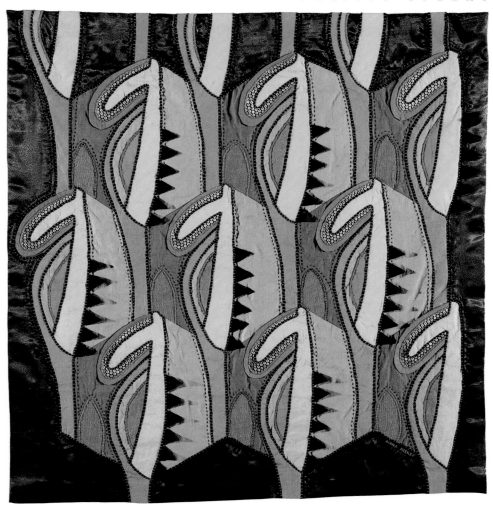

P A C I F I C   U P B E A T

Diana Parkes
Wellington

81cm by 78cm

Cotton lawn, cotton canvas,
synthetics, felt, hand-applique,
couching.

Diana Parkes has been working as a fabric artist for the past 13 years. 'I work in a number of areas. My particular interest is in teaching. I teach hobby classes, advanced classes and workshops throughout New Zealand. My subjects are from the traditional to the very creative. Patchwork has nothing to do with what I do. If the idea I have says it should be constructed by piecing, I will piece it.' The artist designed the wall quilt to hang in her sister's office. 'I had no reason to use that particular design, I had it and wanted to work it. I feel strongly that we have a great deal of inspiration and culture within our Pacific area; I have tried to introduce some of these elements into my work. The strong hammer shapes supported by the dimensional triangles reflect a positive attitude and a feeling of growth.' Diana has always worked with fabrics and thread. 'I enjoyed working with fibres and can't imagine using any other medium. There is plenty out there for me to do yet. The ideas keep flowing through, and I need to keep pushing the boundaries. It is important for both me personally and also in my teaching.'

Anne Patrick
Nelson

147cm by 87cm

Machine-pieced, machine-quilted,
polyester batting, 100% cotton
fabrics, hand-dyed with fibre
reactive and indigo dyes.

Anne says, 'Response to the casual statement "Flying South for the Winter" conjured up visions of vast flocks of migrating birds, which in the hot, hazy summer environment were crisp and clear, but then as the encroaching winter forced the birds south, the roles reversed. The birds became the warmth and the landscape cold, crisp and stark. The ability of colours to evoke responses of warmth and cold, often at the same time like an Indian Summer, has always fascinated me, and added to this, was the work I was doing with colours and their ability to take over, fade out, stand out, contrast or change, depending on the sequential arrangement and the placement of the neighbouring colours. I was also influenced by a book I was reading at the time about the North American Indians, and was struck by the uncomprising fact that most indigenous people have been forced "South" by Western civilisations; and at some point in history a clear takeover has occurred, but often this point is not apparent until later. The quilt from a distance is meant to invite the viewer to get closer and become involved in the many subtleties, such as the colour change sequences from the gradations, that are only apparent upon closer inspection.' Anne feels she is not a producer of work, 'but rather a facilitator of ideas'. 'My area is in the education field. I really enjoy passing on information.'

EGMONT

Jan Pepperell
New Plymouth

48cm by 144cm

Silk, cottons, cotton blends,
compressed needled batting,
machine-pieced.

Jan Pepperell has been stitching since childhood. 'My mother taught embroidery at the local primary school, and when I was a pre-schooler she used to take me along with her and put a needle in my hand. I have always embroidered.' Quiltmaking, Jan sees as an extension of her love of embroidery. She delved into the art eight years ago and has not stopped since. She cites Jinny Beyer as her favourite author. 'Her books make sense, I like her work and her quilts. Her colours really inspire me.' Planning Egmont 'just happened'. 'The mountain is always there, it's the first thing I see each morning, and as a member of the Taranaki Alpine Club, I have climbed it in all seasons. This quilt just had to happen. Stained glass was the ideal medium, piecing or applique would have posed too many problems. The snowline was the only difficulty I had. I had to paint it in.' Jan drew an exact pattern onto her backing fabric and filled in the shapes, from her bulging fabric cupboard. 'Of course as with all quilts, I did not have the right shades of green and had to buy more. I selected ones with texture. Once I get started, I have to work until the project is completed. This quilt was no exception, I completed it in a week. It is one of four in a series. I haven't made the other three yet.' This year Jan packed away her patchwork supplies to concentrate on embroidery and lace making. She says, 'I have already noticed them creeping back in. I plan to continue working in stained glass for a while, although I normally go where it grabs me at the time. I enjoy working with second-hand fabrics but get concerned about ageing problems. I also like stripes. They are so much fun to work with. You can do so much with them – they stretch your mind.'

Clare Plug
Napier

188cm by 122cm

Hand and machine-appliqued,
hand-quilted, cottons, cotton
blends, other fabrics, cotton and
satin piping.

Clare Plug, inspired by the lines, the shapes and the colours present in paua shells, was happy to translate this into fabric. Clare is currently a student at the Napier Polytechnic studying for a Certificate in Craft Design. The course encompasses many mediums which are new to the artist, fibre not being a major subject. She feels that working with materials previously unfamiliar to her has freed her up and influenced her designs. 'I wanted my work to change.' She was keen to do the course as she felt she needed to learn to draw. Taught traditional English piecing by her father in the early seventies, Clare was keen to continue quiltmaking. She saw several exhibitions of antique quilts and visited quilt shops while living overseas. On her return to New Zealand she knew that she wanted to make quilts. Initially self-taught, Clare attended a beginners patchwork course in 1983. The course gave her the range of technical skills she needed. She cites Malcolm Harrison and Jo Cornwall as being influential in her quiltmaking. While working on the project, the artist said she was oblivious to almost everything that was going on around her. As part of the design element of her course, Clare had chosen the paua shell idea for some creative knitting and also for batik. Feeling she had fine-tuned the design, she drew up a full-sized pattern for a quilt. Colours were planned on a small painting and final fabric choices were made as the applique progressed. She says, 'This quilt is an expression of a life-long interest in natural history, especially of New Zealand.'

Faye Quayle says she would have liked to have been a painter, 'but because I sew I am now able to do it with my needle'. Introduced to traditional American Patchwork in 1981, Faye quickly branched into a more contemporary style. She feels seminole patchwork gives her the scope to continue to extend herself. 'I'm open to all new ideas that occur to me. I see everything in patchwork. When I look at something I wonder how I can achieve it with fabric. Quiltmaking inspires me – it is satisfying and relaxing. Colour has no barriers.' 'Sea Garden' is the third in a series of underwater quilts made by Faye. 'I'm inspired by wonderful underwater photographs taken by my son, who scuba dives. I make a point of choosing pictures taken below Pukerua Bay, where I live, and at Kapiti Island, off shore from Pukerua Bay.' Faye, exploring her fondness for curves, began with a four-inch block and experimented with a flexicurve until 'suitably pleasing and representative shapes were defined'. She was delighted when her son commented that she had achieved the distorted view a diver has under water. She says of her quilt, 'Deep in the ocean, fish and other marine life mingle with sponges, drifting seaweed and rocks; a magical underwater garden. Points of silk represent tiny darting fish startled by the diver's intrusion into their world. The unplanned spontaneous quilting lines give the impression of eddies and currents; the movement of the ocean.'

SEA GARDEN

Faye Quayle
Pukerua Bay

MERIT AWARD

101cm square

Cottons, cotton blends, lurex, chintz, silk, wool batting, hand and machine-pieced, hand-appliqued, hand-quilted.

LIFE BEYOND

Janet Ryan
Auckland

82cm by 87cm

Cotton hand-dyed fabrics,
machine and hand-pieced,
hand-appliqued, hand-quilted,
beaded.

When Janet Ryan attended a course in beginners patchwork in 1984, she was immediately hooked. That her fabric collection, which she had started years before was completely unsuitable, did not dampen her enthusiasm. Patchwork and quilting were something for which Janet, a keen home sewer, had been waiting. Working in a quilting shop for two years, and teaching a variety of patchwork, quilting and fabric-craft skills have been an added bonus for her. 'Life Beyond' explored a new area for Janet. Although she has felt drawn to the third dimension for some time, and as early as four years ago attended a Katie Pasquini workshop, it was a subject she did not follow up. She again attended similar classes with Anne Patrick in 1988, but still the work remained a drawingboard project. Janet says, 'I wanted something fast and simple to piece, but my original blocks were boring. I began playing with dimensional graph paper and the quilt just grew.' She experienced numerous difficulties in drawing up the quilt. After discovering that photostat machines can distort when enlarging, Janet enlisted the help of her husband, Kevin. It was he who drew up the templates and designed the quilt centre. The fabrics chosen by Janet were the ones she had dyed herself. A friend rang early one Sunday morning offering her the remains of a dye pot. Janet, not having any suitable fabric on hand, used an old sheet. Due to a busy schedule, Janet was unable to wash the fabric for a further 48 hours. All fabrics had to be cut individually to ensure the colours ran in the correct direction. The quilt was put together like a jigsaw.

'This is the third in a series of quilts using this block. I enjoy arranging my fabrics in colour-tone sequences and then combining these much as one would shuffle a deck of cards. When the blocks are arranged, an interesting interplay of background and foreground can be achieved. I like to think of this type of quilt as a visual playground, with the eye constantly seeking out order – only to have it disappear and turn up somewhere else.'

HOT FLASH

Sue Spigel
Christchurch

125cm square

Cottons, cotton blends, needled polyester batting, machine-pieced, machine-quilted.

LITTLE BOXES

Sue Spigel
Christchurch

100cm by 108cm

Cottons, cotton blends, needled
polyester batting, machine-pieced,
machine-quilted.

'In this quilt I was less concerned with making a pretty quilt and more interested in the manipulation of the basic design. I enjoyed watching the foreground-background shrink and grow with the addition or subtraction of a line or two, and having one's perception shift from hexagons to triangles to boxes and back.' The box block was developed in a workshop conducted by Michael James on two-dimensional design.

'I made this quilt to remind me of my attendance at Symposium '89. The beautiful colours and textures of the Lindisfarne College grounds, where the Symposium was held, inspired my fabric selection. The autumn colours of Hawke's Bay – the reds, browns and golds, are quite different to the seasonal colour changes in my area.' Mary found the design for this quilt in a *Quilters Newsletter Magazine* and altered the pattern slightly for easier piecing. She enjoyed departing from her usual colour palette and was pleased with the movement she achieved through colour and quilting. Mary has held a needle for as long as she can remember and feels patchwork and quilting was a natural progression. Initially self-taught, Mary worked by hand until attending a local class where she discovered machining was not only acceptable, but that it hastened the quiltmaking process. A member of several groups, she says, 'I am interested in both traditional and contemporary quiltmaking and like to do both.'

AUTUMN BREEZE

Mary Transom
Matakana

135cm square

Cotton fabrics, wool batting, machine-pieced, hand-quilted.

' I wanted to make this quilt using the Greenpeace Symbol as a tribute to the group and to their work in New Zealand. I admire Greenpeace as an organisation; I believe they do a lot of good work.' Mary adapted a method from the book *One of a Kind Quilts* by Judy Hopkins to make this quilt. She made an initial plan on graph paper before stitching began. She found she had to use many different blocks for the quilt to work. Some fabrics needed to be hand-dyed to achieve the colour gradation desired. The New Zealand abbreviations in each corner Mary 'wanted to be subtle, a surprise, but in quiet colours'.

P E A C E   S O N G

Mary Transom
Matakana

120cm square

Cotton fabrics, wool batting,
machine-pieced, hand-appliqued,
hand-quilted.

FANTASY IN VIOLET

Lasma Treacher
Auckland

145cm by 100cm

Silks, satins, rayons, polyesters,
tulle, cottons, metallic thread,
beads, sequins, braids, needled
polyester batting, machine-pieced,
machine-appliqued,
hand-embellished,
hand-embroidered.

Lasma Treacher, a graduate from the Wellington Polytechnic School of Textile Design, believes the tactile nature of fabric is what attracts her to quiltmaking. 'I used to paint. My water colours sold well but I was never overly enthused about them and I got bored with painting. I have always had a feeling for textiles, and love playing with fabrics and wool. I feel very comfortable with them. To know I am going to spend the day working with fabric gives me instant pleasure. Fabrics are so close to you while you are working with them. Fabrics make me come alive.' 'Fantasy in Violet' was inspired by Lasma's wish to convey her passion for combinations of colour, texture and lustre of fabrics in a pleasing and seductive way. She started with small sketches and fabric combinations. The lady combines the features of two friends who modelled for the project. Lasma feels the quilt was a 'hit and miss affair'. 'I sewed the crazy patches onto the background fabric and then I laid on my lady. I wanted the richness of the fabrics to be in contact with my fantasy person. I had to play around a lot to get the skin tone and translucence I desired. I wanted her to come alive. To me this quilt is a piece exploring the use of textiles and embellishments to give richness and light. Butterflies to me have special meaning – I use them to represent freedom.'

' I was inspired by the Amish use of colour and challenged myself to use colours like yellow, which I do not particularly enjoy working with. I wanted one colour to move from light to dark and the other to move from dark to light. The colours remind me of a stormy autumn sky. The quilting began as wind currents, but now, to me, it resembles leaves.' Although Brenda was brought up with a quiltmaking grandmother and mother, she feels that her real awareness of the art only developed when she moved to New Zealand. She attended lessons in Christchurch given by a tutor who only taught English piecing methods. 'That is why I probably still do a large amount of paper-piecing. I tend to be fairly disorganised and, with American piecing you have to be accurate and measure everything. Providing I cut my papers correctly, I have no problems with this method. I like the action of hand-piecing and hand-quilting. My inspiration comes from the fabrics. I like to use plain materials or to find prints that nobody else is using. I'm beginning to paint my own fabrics to titivate my large collection of plains and to have something different in my collection. I'm obsessed with quiltmaking. I suppose I haven't found another way of using my creativity.'

AMISH AUTUMN

Brenda Visser
Christchurch

74cm square

Cottons, cotton blends, lurex, hand-painted fabric, needled polyester batting, machine-pieced, hand-quilted.

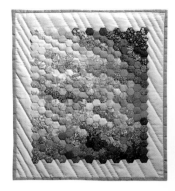

Brenda Visser
Christchurch

38cm by 33cm each
(four pieces)

Cottons, cotton blends,
satins, lurex, needled
polyester batting,
paper-pieced, hand-quilted.

'I made "Amish Autumn" first and thoroughly enjoyed the process so decided to make a quilt for each season. I cut out a large number of fabric hexagons and played with these until I was satisfied with the way they looked. To me the four pieces demonstrate the quite subtle changes of colour from one season to the next in Canterbury. There would be greater contrasts, especially in winter, if I had followed the colours of my native Canada.'

Mariya Waters was delighted that her quilt, 'Time Warp' was, when completed, exactly as she imagined it. This, her second quilt, was designed on a scrap of paper while sitting with her father, a patient in an intensive care ward. She says, 'Time was important to me. I had to keep myself occupied. During a break from the ward, I saw a poster advertising the quiltmaking competition. There was, at the time, a lot of information available regarding the coming 1990 Sesqui Centennial, with the theme "New Zealand in Time". This inspired me to design my quilt.' Transferring the design to fabrics posed some problems for Mariya. The desired colour tones required her first experiments with fabric dyeing. The quilt top was machine-pieced but the results were less than satisfactory. She unpicked the whole of the top and pieced it by hand. Mariya says of her quilt, 'It combines the modern concept of a time warp with events which have occurred in New Zealand. The English, represented by paper-piecing; the Maori, the blue sky and the quilted green plants. The colour pink is, to me, a colour of friendship. I added white for peace and red for love. All of these are mixed together in time – from the traditional concepts to the contemporary, the Maori and the European. The light at the end of the tunnel is the unknown time to come. Overall, the quilt says time is important – it is the continuous thread of our nation.' Mariya has always worked with fabric and thread. For several years she designed a range of fashion knitwear garments for under-fours. Although this is only her second quilt, she has a love of the art, especially the more contemporary and has over the years, devoured many quilting books. Currently fully employed and doing three papers at university, Mariya looks forward to a time when she can devote herself to further fabric art.

TIME WARP

Mariya Waters
Wellington

108cm by 106cm

Cottons, cotton blends, needled polyester batting, hand-pieced, hand-quilted.

91

Penny Wenlock first heard of the Enzed Sewing National Quiltmaking Competition two months before the entry deadline. Always keen to make a large quilt, she decided to enter. Finally locating an entry form in February, she realised she had only ten days to complete the quilt. 'It was a day and night project,' said Penny. 'I'm an artist but the need to contribute to the family income means that I make quilted patchwork clothes for children which I sell at markets and craft shows throughout New Zealand.' Penny does not consider herself a quiltmaker, but rather as someone experienced with cloth and design. This is the largest project she has worked on. When asked how she planned the project, Penny said, 'I started at the top and I knew something would happen. I did not make a sketch. Each day I take my son to school, a drive of 20 kilometres. We live in a bay and we have to rise up over 2000 feet through layers of hills. From the top we view the mountains to the north and west and the sea to the east stretching as far south as the Antarctic. I make this journey every school day in all weathers and seasons. I see my quilt as a banner mirroring the landscape of New Zealand.' Discussing the project with a local potter, Craig Fletcher, it was decided that he would supply ceramic fish and birds to embellish the quilt. These are attached to the cloth with silk, indicating that the wildlife is tied to the landscape but retains independence or freedom. Penny says, 'I have a love of cloth and a desire to sew. I like to be able to paint with my sewing machine.'

Penny Wenlock and
Craig Fletcher
Little River, Banks Peninsula

240cm by 285cm

Machine-pieced, cotton fabrics, silks, calico, ceramics.

Penelope Whitaker
Alexandra

186cm by 146cm

Cotton fabrics, needled polyester
batting, machine-pieced,
hand-quilted.

Kashmir-born and English-reared, Penelope Whitaker was at first, a reluctant patchworker. 'I was roped in by a group of friends. I could hardly thread a needle and did what I did in a desultory fashion. Suddenly I found I could use fabric in a most satisfying way. I became really keen. I was able to express my ideas and feelings in quiltmaking in a way I was unable to in any other medium.' Although Penelope has lived in New Zealand since 1949, she has had a continuing interest in Islamic design, particularly weaving. 'Kashmir in Mind' is a response to her ongoing attraction to this area. The quilt was designed on graph paper, and Penelope found it necessary to dye some fabrics to achieve the desired shades. 'I was delighted to find that Jinny Beyer fabrics were inspired by Indian designs. They had the exact feel I wanted. It was as though she had designed them especially for me.' She says of her quilt, 'This is an interpretation, in basic patchwork techniques, of the type of design found in Islamic Prayer rugs. It has a pale central field the shape of a Mihrab which is surrounded by darkening bands of brown set with tile-like blocks in unrepeating colour combinations. Forty-two different fabrics were used to give depth and interest to the subdued colour scheme.' The artist works in many ways within the medium. She has a special fondness for strip-piecing and is fascinated with the design potential of this method.

S A F A R I

Betty Wilson
Matakana

130cm by 106cm

A hundred percent cotton fabrics,
polyester batting, machine-pieced,
machine-quilted.

Introduced to Traditional English Patchwork in 1981, Betty Wilson finally found a use for the two suitcases of fabric scraps she had refused to part with. Although she was told patchwork was not patchwork if done by machine, she quickly adapted to the methods taught and immediately began work on her first quilt – a queensize which she hand-quilted on a floor frame designed by her husband. 'I always knew I would make a quilt. I branched out into my own designs soon after starting quiltmaking. I didn't like the thought of copying the designs of others and I wanted to be different.' 'Safari' was inspired by a fabric Betty purchased in Hawaii. She regrets using the leftover scraps on the reverse of the quilt and laments that she has none left for other projects. She says, ' I had an idea of using the whole zebra but I couldn't make it work. Once I had cut up the zebras, I designed the quilt as I went. The quilt was laid out on the floor and over a few days I rearranged it several times until I felt satisfied with the design. The effect I wanted was of animal tracks through a wilderness but blending into the background. I wanted a little subtle colour to depict flowers and vines. The snail trail in non-traditional colours suited the idea and helped the combination of jungle prints with parts of the zebra bodies.' Betty is rapidly making a name for herself in the field of pieced clothing. Fourteen years ago she said she would not make any more clothing, having spent years dressmaking for her six children. 'I wanted to try something different. Clothing challenges me and I find garments sell more easily. They are "one off" and people like that.'